DESIGNING

with PLANTS

fine
Gardening Design Guides

DESIGNING
with PLANTS

Creative Ideas *from* America's Best Gardeners

The Taunton Press

Special thanks to the editors, art directors, copy editors, and other staff members of Fine Gardening *who contributed to the development of the articles in this book.*

Front cover photographers: Lee Anne White, © The Taunton Press, Inc. (large); Steve Silk, © The Taunton Press, Inc. (inset)
Back cover photographers: Steve Silk, © The Taunton Press, Inc. (large); Bard Wrigley (Erica Glasener photo); all other photos courtesy *Fine Gardening* magazine, © The Taunton Press, Inc.
Publisher: Jim Childs
Acquisitions Editor: Lee Anne White
Editorial Assistant: Meredith DeSousa
Technical Editor: Todd Meier
Copy Editor: Candace Levy
Indexer: Linda Stannard
Art Director: Paula Schlosser
Design Manager: Rosalind Wanke
Cover and Interior Designer: Lori Wendin
Layout Artist: Susan Fazekas

Taunton
BOOKS & VIDEOS
for fellow enthusiasts

Printed in the United States of America
10 9 8 7 6 5 4 3 2 1

The Taunton Press, Inc., 63 South Main Street, PO Box 5506,
Newtown, CT 06470-5506
e-mail: tp@taunton.com

Distributed by Publishers Group West

Library of Congress Cataloging-in-Publication Data
Designing with plants : creative ideas from America's best gardeners.
p. cm.—(Fine gardening design guides)
ISBN 1-56158-472-X
1. Plants, Ornamental. 2. Gardens—Designs. 3. Landscape gardening.
4. Plants, Ornamental—United States. 5. Gardens—United States—Design.
6. Landscape gardening—United States. I. Fine gardening. II. Series.
SB407.D42 2001
712—dc21   00-059934

"*I spend my summers going through the catalogs, making notes of what I want to plant in the fall. I make lists and then tear them up and start over again. I want everything I see, and it is so hard to choose."*

—Elizabeth Lawrence,
Through the Garden Gate

Contents

Introduction

For most, making great plant combinations is one of the most thrilling aspects of gardening. There's nothing quite like the satisfaction of hearing the "oohs" and "aahs" of friends when they spot one of your most successful plantings. There are, of course, classic plant combinations that almost never fail—like roses and clematis (providing they bloom at the same time). But we need not stick strictly to classic combinations. As long as we first meet a plant's cultural needs, we can mix and match as we choose.

When we create plantings, we call on our artistic skills. We can be studied or flamboyant—paying close attention to foliage details or mixing flower colors with abandon. And like any art form, what works and what doesn't is often a matter of personal taste. But whether we're trying to make a bold, colorful statement or create a simple, serene setting, there are, fortunately, some basic rules of composition to guide us along the way. By understanding these principles, we can improve our garden design skills and gain enough confidence to know when to break the rules.

In *Designing with Plants*, some of America's top garden designers share their secrets for placing plants effectively in the garden—whether it's making eye-catching perennial combinations, creating an allée or espalier, or choosing the right plants for special places. For years, they've been sharing their insights in *Fine Gardening* magazine. Now you have their work in a single book that you can take with you out in the garden for inspiration and ideas.

DESIGN
TECHNIQUES

1

PICTURE THE DELICATE, FEATHERY FOLIAGE of ferns against the big, bold leaves of hostas. Masses of fountain-shaped ornamental grasses with their fading, hay-colored flowers juxtaposed against mounding, rusty-colored clumps of *Sedum* 'Autumn Joy'. Or the striking, globe-shaped giant allium (*Allium giganteum*) growing up from a ground-hugging, finely foliaged Japanese maple. This is what planting design is all about.

While combining plants liberates the artist in most of us, it helps to know a few basic techniques of planting design. And though we may first think about flower color when making stunning combinations, it is important to keep in mind that most plants only flower for a short period of time. Form, size, and texture are just as important. So in this section, we'll cover the basics of planting design, review the role of massed plantings in the landscape, and explore a few creative pruning techniques that teach us to see the form and potential in plants.

DOUGLAS RUHREN

is a garden designer and horticultural consultant in Durham, North Carolina. He designed many of the borders at nearby Montrose, the Daniel Stowe Botanical Garden, and Denver Botanic Gardens.

Design Techniques

for Picturesque Plantings

(FAR LEFT) Keep color schemes simple. Yellow and violet are repeated throughout this border, with orange as an occasional accent.

(INSET) Make the most of see-through plants like this purple *Verbena bonariensis*, which contrasts in color with a yellow canna.

FROM CULTIVARS AND KITSCH to garden accessories and art, these days you can find just about anything you're looking for, and then some, at garden centers, in mail-order catalogs, through seed exchanges, and on the Internet. So, just what does a gardener do when faced with this seemingly endless array of materials? How does one put the pieces together to create a coherent and attractive garden?

As a garden designer, I have three basic design rules that guide my decisions, especially when it comes to selecting and combining plants. First, balance contrast and repetition. Second, use restraint when combining colors. And finally, pay as much attention to texture, shape, size, and form as you do to color when placing plants, structures, and ornaments in a garden.

Think of flowers and foliage when using complementary colors. The deep-burgundy foliage of smokebush looks nice with the pinkish flowers of Joe Pye weed.

Same color, different shape. By contrasting leaf shapes and plant forms, you can show distinction between similarly colored plants like this variegated red twig dogwood and eulalia grass.

CONTRAST CREATES EXCITEMENT, WHILE REPETITION HOLDS A DESIGN TOGETHER

I have come to believe that creating a successful design or composition requires finding the right balance between contrast and repetition. Just what this balance might be is not set in stone; it will vary with what the artist—in our case, a garden designer—is trying to communicate.

Contrast is any visual aspect that two elements, when seen together, do not have in common. Often something is only noticed, or is more strikingly noticed, when it is contrasted with another element. For instance, the delicate, lacy foliage of a maidenhair fern (*Adiantum pedatum*) stands out much stronger against the large, bold leaves of a hosta than it does with another small-leaved plant like bleeding heart (*Dicentra eximia*). Contrast adds excitement to a combination: too little and the design bores; too much and the fainthearted swoon. The choice is yours to make, somewhere along the continuum from restful to overly exciting. But remember, with too many contrasts, the design can lack focus and lose its impact.

Repetition might sound boring, but it is absolutely essential to successful design. Repetition is what holds a design together and prevents a design from being an endless series of individual plants (all contrasts). Repetition of certain elements can also move the eye through the landscape, creating a visual rhythm in the placement of plants and other elements. Certain plants might be repeated, as

Repeat the form and change the color. The large, oval leaves of hostas create unity in this shady border, even though the foliage color changes.

can forms, textures, or colors. Examples might include repeated masses of one plant throughout the garden, or repetition of a particular form—say, the strong conical or columnar form of certain shrubs, or shrubs sheared to this form—or a color scheme in which a number of colors are repeated throughout. Repetition of an element can make its use seem intentional rather than accidental. In simpler terms, it looks as if it belongs.

IT HELPS TO LIMIT YOUR COLOR PALETTE

Color is often the first element considered by a designer. Too often, it is the only one considered. For many reasons, designing is easy if the only goal is to have a colorful garden. Nurseries offer us a wider—and ever-widening—selection of plants than ever before, and many plants are also available in a broader range of colors. For instance, garden phlox (*Phlox paniculata*), once readily recognized by its purple-pink flowers, is now available in the coral-orange of 'Orange Perfection', the red-violet of 'Albert Leo Schlageter', the saturated purple-

violet of 'The King', and the red of 'Starfire', among others.

And then there is foliage color. Lots of new colors and numerous forms of variegation are available now. Just this year, I found variegated sports of *Cuphea ignea* and *Crinum* × *powellii* 'Ellen Bosanquet'. Soon, it will be easy to garden without green at all, which I'm sure will initiate the heyday of all-green gardens.

Repeat a single striking plant throughout the garden to tie it all together. Here, a variegated grass lights the way down a shady path.

"Most unsuccessful designs fail not in the use of color, but in the use of texture."

I don't believe there are any bad colors—just bad use of color. So what does one do with this easily acquired abundance of color? First, select a limited color scheme—one that is something less than the full spectrum. Limiting the range of colors reduces the contrasts, but repeating the selected few colors gives a stronger impact and coherence to the design. It can also set one garden apart from another, which is especially useful if your site consists of a series of beds or borders.

The most commonly used division of garden color separates the warm (red, orange, and yellow) and cool (violet, blue, and green) ends of the spectrum. Or, colors can be arranged according to their value—the degree of saturation of the pigment. This approach is based on the combination of highly saturated colors (rich tones like orange and magenta) or less saturated tones (a scheme of pastel colors). Smaller divisions of either group can be made with just one or two colors. Rarely is a color scheme truly monochromatic since there is usually the green of foliage. Indeed, what strikes me most strongly in the red garden at England's famous Hidcote Manor is the green of the foliage, which creates such striking contrast with the reds.

Many designers suggest that, in a two-color (dichromatic) scheme, one color should dominate and the other should act as a repeated contrast to it, rather than both colors being used in equal amounts. Having now worked with both blue-and-yellow and purple-and-orange color schemes, I have yet to determine the correct balance between repeating and contrasting colors. I have come to believe, though, that a color scheme limited to one or two colors can be awfully flat, and that it can

Vary foliage shapes and plant forms. This is especially important when working with a monochromatic color scheme like this white border.

be jazzed up with the accents of a contrasting color. At Hidcote, the true blue of Salvia guarantica brings the red garden to life. In the purple-and-orange garden I designed, the contrast comes from the glaucous foliage of tree tobacco (*Nicotiana glauca*), switch grass (*Panicum virgatum* 'Heavy Metal'), and *Echeveria secunda* var. *glauca*. Accent colors are akin to jewelry worn to spice up one's attire.

Finally, one need not adhere slavishly to a color scheme. For example, the color scheme of one garden can change over the seasons. Indeed, we can see this in nature, with the preponderance of pinkish purples in spring, and violets and golden yellows in late summer and fall.

CONTRAST BOLD AND FINE-TEXTURED PLANTS FOR VISUAL RELIEF

Having said so much about color, perhaps the most important point I'd make about designing a garden is that it's not just about color. Most unsuccessful designs fail not in the use of color, but in the use of texture. Usually the problem is too much fine texture and not enough bold texture.

Too much fine texture imparts a weak, soft, unfocused effect, while bold texture can provide relief from an excess of unstructured fluff. In fact, the two are most exciting in contrast to each other. Bold contrast in the garden can be provided by large-leaved plants, such as cannas, hostas, or rice paper plant (*Tetrapanax papyrifer*), or by plants of distinctive form, such as yuccas or shrubs sheared into geometric shapes. Gardens are more than just plants, and a large pot, sculpture, or garden structure can also provide relief from too much fine-textured foliage.

On the other hand, vegetation can visually soften an overabundance of hard, geometric

lines from paths and walls. Often this contrast between the manmade and the natural results in a juxtaposition of formal and informal elements in the garden. Though I was taught that the use of the "formal" in garden design was practically a sin, I have come to enjoy the contrast and interplay between formal and informal elements. The two highlight each other. I can think of no better example than the delightfully shocking contrast of Christopher Lloyd's new tropical garden juxtaposed against his father's topiary pheasants atop their yew pyramids.

GROUP PLANTS AS NATURE MIGHT

Typically, the size of a site's manmade objects determines the overall size of the garden and the scale of the masses of plants used in it.

Contrast in flower shape is just as dramatic as contrast in foliage shape. This *Triteleia laxa* 'Koningin Fabiola' and sea holly make a striking pair.

Use small plants in masses, as nature might. Love-in-a-mist and lavender spread in drifts among blue oat grass, golden creeping oregano, and daylilies.

A modest cottage might be well complemented by a busy jumble of a garden, but a larger home or building calls for a bolder design. This doesn't mean that only big plants may be employed around big structures; smaller plants can be used, too, but in sufficiently large masses or drifts.

In other instances, mature trees can help to determine an appropriate scale. That ring of crocuses around the trunk of a mature oak will always look ridiculous, while a drift of many hundreds of them is more in scale.

"Typically, the size of a site's manmade objects determines the overall size of the garden and the scale of the masses of plants used in it."

Chosen plants should be used in a range of different-sized masses appropriate to the site, with a few smaller masses as contrasts. Indeed, a few plants can be used individually as accents, as vegetative exclamation points. I urge the use of at least a few bold plants even in the smallest gardens, for they add a drama that tiny plants (which might seem better in scale with the space) never can.

I like to arrange masses as nature might in a wildflower meadow, with several large masses representing where a species first seeded, accompanied by smaller outlying colonies, so that it looks as if they had self-sown from the original mass. The larger masses are placed as focal points; the smaller masses provide the repetition, and help to carry the eye through the whole composition. The individual masses are of irregular outline; I like to think of them as clouds or drifts.

One of the effects I hope to achieve is that the masses of different species consort comfortably with each other, yet provide enough contrast so that each is shown to its best advantage. The look that I absolutely hope to avoid is that of an earlier style of herbaceous perennial border, with rigid blocks of solid color bumping almost noisily, even gratingly, up against each other—all contrast with no repetition.

USE VERTICAL PLANTS TO PIERCE MOUNDS OF ROUNDED PLANTS

Another element you can contrast or repeat is form or shape—whether of objects, or of plants or their parts. There can be beauty and interest in the foliage, stems, buds, fruit, and the overall habit of a plant. After all, a garden is not just flowers.

It is good to design with this in mind, because most plants bloom for only a brief period. Siberian iris (*Iris sibirica*), for instance, is an elegant foliage plant all summer, unlike most bearded irises, whose foliage often languishes after flowering, especially in humid climates. If the Siberian iris is an older, fertile variety such as 'Caesar's Brother' (most newer hybrids are sterile), the rich brown seedpods are also handsome through the winter. If we place less emphasis on flower color and more on the texture, shape, and other features of plants, our enjoyment of gardens becomes richer and more subtle.

Plants of strongly vertical shape—such as irises, gladioli, and many grasses—bring delightful relief from the amorphous mounding masses of most plants—such as geraniums, say, or *Lantana*. Using vertical plants to pierce the masses of their mounding neighbors helps avoid what I think of as the "school-picture

syndrome," where the shortest plants are backed by a series of ever taller plants, which lets us see only their heads. Some plants also have pretty shoulders, torsos, and legs; they need space around them to be seen. And bring forward some taller, "see-through" plants like *Verbena bonariensis* and *Nicotiana langsdorffii*—the contrasts will delight.

So be bold and adventurous. Have fun. And remember: Garden design is a very personal art; there are no hard-and-fast rules.

Sheathes of iris foliage pierce mounds of asters to create a striking late-summer composition in the perennial border.

Mass

RUTH ADAMS

served as managing editor for *The New York Botanical Garden Illustrated Encyclopedia of Horticulture*. She studied commercial horticulture and land-scape design at the New York Botanical Garden.

Plantings
Make a Bold
Statement

Seen from a distance, sweeps of textural plants resemble a tap-estry. Low-growing blue rug juniper (*Juniperus horizontalis* 'Wiltonii') gracefully mingles with selections of *Sedum* and silver-mound artemisia.

I LEARNED ABOUT THE VALUE of mass plant-ings when my husband and I bought a renovated barn with a large backyard opening to a 3-acre hay field. I liked the fact that our site enjoyed full sun and a magnificent view of mountains, but I was stumped initially by this new gardening challenge. I knew that traditional English perennial beds would not suit the architecture of the barnlike house and that a cottage gar-den would be dwarfed by the vista.

So I turned to some principles of Japanese gardening. I tried to identify with the pervading spirit of the site, use its strengths, and, most of all, remain sensitive to the exist-ing scale. Given our location, it made sense to place the garden between the expansive view and the house. Mass plantings of low-growing plants seemed the best way to achieve harmony between the garden and the surrounding landscape. These plantings complement, rather than com-pete with, the natural panorama and can be enjoyed both

Accentuate colorful foliage plants by growing them en masse. A ribbon of purple sage (*Salvia officinalis* 'Purpurascens') makes an attractive edging.

Repetition of a single plant can create a sense of unity. Masses of blue oat grass are repeated throughout the garden.

close up and from a distance. Well-placed mass plantings in any setting can draw the eye and lend a naturalistic air to a garden.

EVALUATE THE ROLE OF MASS IN YOUR LANDSCAPE

In gardening terms, mass refers to a body of coherent plantings, usually of indefinite shape and often of considerable size. It can be creat-

ed by grouping several pots of the same plant or several plants that have similar color, texture, and density. For example, two or three plants that bloom at the same time in a similar color can form a mass. Or several varieties of grasses—even of varying heights—can be combined to make a bold statement.

Since mass is a relative term, it must be developed in relation to other elements— architectural structures, other plantings (such as a shrub hedge), or even open lawn. Looking at the surroundings of my future garden helped in determining an appropriate sense of scale. First, I considered the ratio of the proposed garden (when viewed from the house or terrace) to the imposing backdrop of field, forest, and mountain range. Thinking "big," I tried to balance the massive scale of the site by breaking up the sloping, rectangular lawn with a 50-ft. by 70-ft. pond. This also solved the dilemma of what to do with a gaping hole filled with several huge boulders left behind by the previous owners. We moved the rocks and placed them around the pond.

This became a perfect setting for massed plantings. For example, around the side of the pond closest to the house, I planted only low-growing junipers (*Juniperus* spp.) and cotoneasters (*Cotoneaster* spp.). Viewed from a distance, these plantings appear as broad sweeps.

KEEP MASSES IN PROPORTION

Proportion is key to determining how many plants to mass in an area. For example, in a spot roughly 100 square ft. on the far side of the pond, I planted clusters of four different plants—two varieties of *Sedum*, silvermound artemisia (*Artemisia schmidtiana*), and snow-in-summer (*Cerastium tomentosum*). The effect of these combined forms, textures, and colors is akin to the muted shadings of a tapestry.

"Well-placed mass plantings in any setting can draw the eye and lend a naturalistic air to a garden."

I alternated these ground-cover masses with low-growing focal points: standards of *Juniperus procumbens* 'Nana' and weeping trees such as Norway spruce (*Picea abies* 'Pendula'), katsura tree (*Cercidyphyllum japonicum* f. *pendulum*), and Eastern hemlock (*Tsuga canadensis* 'Pendula'). They add height and definition to the planting area's boundaries.

I've also found that smaller gardens, or smaller spaces in large gardens, can usually handle some massing of plants. In a walk-in bed behind the pond—about 10 ft. wide by

Create a hedge with two dense layers of perennials. A row of black-eyed Susans is backed by a dwarf fountain grass.

> *"When planting in masses, the goal is to see broad sweeps rather than insignificant patches of color and texture."*

35 ft. long—I planted drifts of colorful perennials that draw the eye through the path. As a general rule, I used not fewer than five pots of the same perennial in a section, and in most cases I used 7 to 13. I made exceptions for big plants, such as *Nepeta* 'Six Hills Giant' and *Crambe cordifolia*. The number of plants I choose, and how I group them, is ultimately determined by eye. Whenever possible, I opt for a naturalistic, flowing style.

In keeping with the open-field style of the landscape, I included prairie plants such as coneflowers (*Echinacea* spp.), bee balms (*Monarda* spp.), and monkshoods (*Aconitum* spp.) punctuated with blue oat grass (*Helictotrichon sempervirens*). I especially like the hedgelike effect created by a band of black-eyed Susans (*Rudbeckia fulgida* var. *sullivantii* 'Goldsturm') backed by a dwarf fountain grass (*Pennisetum alopecuroides* 'Hameln').

USE MASSES TO ACCENTUATE COLOR OR TEXTURE

When planting in masses, the goal is to see broad sweeps rather than insignificant patches of color and texture. Many low-growing perennials look appealing en masse. For example, groupings of plants with textured foliage, such as junipers, heaths (*Erica* spp.), and heathers (*Calluna vulgaris*) make excellent foundation plantings when informal, curving lines are desired. And spreaders like dead nettle (*Lamium maculatum* 'White Nancy') and wild ginger (*Asarum canadense*) are wonderful ground covers beneath trees.

Taller plants can help create a balanced sense of scale along with groupings of shorter perennials. For prairie-style screens or see-through hedges, mass tall native plants such as Joe Pye weed (*Eupatorium fistulosum* 'Gateway') in combinations with grasses such as species of *Miscanthus*. For a dramatic effect in a woodland area, group large numbers of ostrich ferns (*Matteuccia struthiopteris*), Japanese painted ferns (*Athyrium niponicum*), or hostas.

Lackluster plantings, especially shrubs, also can become the basis for creating a mass. One way is to simply plant more of an existing plant or type of plant. For example, a spindly row of lilacs can be transformed into a billowy cloud of color and scent by adding new plants among the established ones. For shrub masses that offer fall and winter interest, plant large clusters of Japanese hollies (*Ilex crenata*) or Sawara false cypress (*Chamaecyparis pisifera*).

Space plants to allow for mature growth. The author lays out a large bed of heaths and heathers in which she interspersed a few juniper and cypress plants.

I also create drifts by filling in spaces between existing plants. I designed a hot border on one side of the lawn by using a spotty arrangement of a dozen or so peonies (*Paeonia* spp.) as the backdrop for sweeps of plants with foliage or blooms in shades of deep red, yellow, and white.

USE ANNUALS AS FILLERS

It's often difficult to create a finished-looking garden while waiting for plants to mature. Massing annuals around slower-growing plants is a simple way to overcome this challenge. Statuesque plants like *Nicotiana sylvestris* can add sculptural shapes until new shrubs mature. Ground-hugging annuals will fill in gaps between newly planted perennials and, if they self-seed, can contribute elements of unpredictability and excitement year after year. Given the ever-increasing selections of annuals available, it's easy to find suitable companions. And, because perennial gardens often lose their luster in the dog days of summer, planting annuals can be a perfect way to perk up the beds. It's fun to experiment with annuals because the presentation can always be changed the following year.

Plant perennials in groups of five or more for eye-catching appeal. This bed features masses of balloon flowers (*Platycodon gradiflorus*), blazing star (*Liatris spicata*), and black-eyed Susans.

MARILYN RAFF

owns a landscape design, installation, and maintenance business. She is active in the North American Rock Garden Society and teaches at the Denver Botanic Gardens.

A Tapestry *of* Textures

Ornamental grasses with dramatically different growth habits give this setting plenty of visual texture. The upright feather reed grass and billowy hairy brome are accented by the prickly foliage and flowers of a sea holly.

I YEARN FOR A GARDEN whose beauty lasts all year, a garden filled with eye-appealing combinations that lure me from one spot to the next. I've searched far and wide for ways to bring this special magic to my garden, and I've looked in some unusual places. Some of my ideas are drawn from psychology and alchemy, the sciences of change and transformation. Alchemy, dating from the Middle Ages, was an early form of chemistry. Its practitioners invoked mystical and natural powers in an effort to change lead and other base metals into gold. By combining two or more simple, raw materials, medieval alchemists sought to create an entirely different element, an alloy more enchanting and exciting than the sum of its parts.

That's what I try to do in my garden with plants and other materials. Alchemy is a wonderful metaphor for gardening. By mixing and contrasting diverse plants and their parts—including leaves, stems, and seed heads—I can

A candelabra-shaped mullien with big leaves shows off its soft, fuzzy texture.

Ornamental grasses are often spiky, both in looks and to the touch.

Tiny pea gravel contrasts with the smooth surface of larger boulders.

Boulders create a recurring textural theme that helps tie the garden together.

A plant's contribution can change over time, from soft foliage in spring to frothy flowers in summer.

refashion a lovely garden picture and, I hope, create a new composition that's worth its weight in gold.

OPPOSITES ARE ATTRACTIVE

I like plants with dynamic visual appeal: dramatic foliage, beautiful silky flowers, spiky seed heads. A plant with any one of these qualities is lovely by itself. But over the years, I've learned the real beauty of a garden lies in its combinations, and that a single lovely plant becomes an even more dramatic player when placed near another plant or object that is in some way its visual opposite. Placing something rough next to something smooth, something large next to something small, or even something round next to something linear, creates a dramatic juxtaposition. Now I even use parts of the hardscape to enhance my textural garden compositions. Boulders, unusual pots, and gravel paths all play roles in the visually rich textures at the heart of my garden.

One of my favorite ways to create visual texture is to combine plants in ways that emphasize and dramatize their differences. Putting a towering plant with large foliage, like plume poppy (*Macleaya cordata*), next to something that snuggles against the ground with very tiny leaves, like pussytoes (*Antennaria parvifolia*), for example, dramatizes their differences and creates a spirited pairing.

The principle of pairing opposites also holds true for any grouping of plants based on radically different features, whether it is size, shape, or habit. This can be especially effective with ornamental grasses. I placed the upright plumes of feather reed grass (*Calamagrostis acutiflora* 'Karl Foerster') next to a billowy clump of hairy brome (*Bromus ramosus*). Although both grasses are about the same shade of tan late in the season, their strikingly different silhouettes—one drooping and one

"I like plants with dynamic visual appeal: dramatic foliage, beautiful silky flowers, spiky seed heads."

Delicate, lacy textures lend an airy touch to more architectural foliage. The feathery fronds of Russian pincushion (*Phuopsis stylosa*) lighten the dark leaves and berries of Russian hawthorn (*Crataegus ambigua*).

Seedpods add late-season splendor to combinations. The seedpods of love-in-a-mist create a dramatic background for the blooms of a blanket flower.

Juxtapose large and small plants for drama. Putting a towering plant with large foliage, like plume poppy, next to something finely textured and ground hugging, like pussytoes, creates a spirited pairing.

USE ALL PARTS OF A PLANT, FROM STEMS TO SEED HEADS

My garden reinvents itself as spring, summer, and fall progress, creating vibrant snapshots of plants in different phases of their seasonal cycles. At one time of year, a plant's contribution to the garden picture may be its fuzzy leaves or thorny stems, at another, it may be soft, delicate flowers. Later still, it may be prickly seed heads.

Love-in-a-mist (*Nigella damascena*) is the perfect example of a plant that's constantly evolving to create new compositions. With ferny foliage, frilly looking flowers, and, later in the season, spiky, swollen seedpods, its ever-changing features can play all sorts of roles. Using it with blanket flower (*Gaillardia* spp.) creates an interesting effect. Though they are both round, the cool, prickly looking love-in-a-mist seedpods and the warm, sensuous blanket flower blossoms are strikingly different. The contrasts between the two invite inspection.

Grasses add great interest and form to the garden, and can be contrasted with other plants in large or small scale. But I find them just as useful for their delicate seed heads. The seed heads of most grasses are an airy, feathery finale to the growing season and bring a sense of fragility to pairings with more sturdy, architectural foliage. The airy, wandlike seed heads of sheep's fescue (*Festuca ovina*) offer dramatic contrast against the more intricate leaves of a bloody cranesbill (*Geranium sanguineum*) and fast-spreading cypress spurge (*Euphorbia cyparissias*).

PUT THE HARDSCAPE TO WORK TOO

My garden's hardscape—gravel paths, smooth ceramic containers, and rugged-looking boulders—also plays a role in creating visual textures. Just as with plants, the key is combining the visual "feel" of these elements—their hard-

staunchly vertical—make a pleasing pairing. A cluster of prickly looking, blue orbs of flat sea holly (*Eryngium planum*) next to the grasses adds another textural element to the composition.

Varying plant height also contributes to dynamic garden compositions. In my garden, I've emphasized contrasts in size by placing clusters of small, detail-rich plants against a background panorama of tall plants with bold, textural features.

"As much as I like the play of opposites in my garden, I'm careful to avoid introducing too much contrast and busyness."

ness, smoothness, or coarse texture—with something that looks dramatically different.

In one spot of the garden, I placed a smooth, twine-draped, clay vessel next to a gravel path, where the roughness of the tiny stones plays against the sleek look of the pot. To add even richer textures, I planted the area with borage (*Borago officinalis*), whose fuzzy foliage brings softness to the composition. Even the colors work—the blue of the borage, the burnt orange of the pot, and the tawny hues of the gravel create a solidly earthy palette. I see the union of these many opposites as an electrifying alchemical event. Each element draws on the other, making this a splendid garden moment.

I even use the boulders that crop up here and there in my garden to help link my plantings visually. They add a sense of the ageless, and their solidity provides a resting place for the eye against the bustle of foliage and flower that enriches so much of the garden. To me, the stones and the tufts of grass I plant near them tie my garden into a cohesive whole by creating a recurring, textural theme.

The stones play another, more cerebral role for me. I garden near Denver, Colorado, and the boulders have a rugged, inorganic character that makes the overlay of living plants seem even more magical. It's almost like a microcosm of my Rocky Mountain surroundings.

PRACTICE THE FINE ART OF RESTRAINT

As much as I like the play of opposites in my garden, I'm careful to avoid introducing too much contrast and busyness. That only creates confusion and a visual mess. Instead, I work to create something with more subtlety, and look for a gentle alliance between hardscape and plants, something that looks more like a graceful dance than a wild fling. Finding that balance can be hard, but I've learned to trust my eye, my feelings, and my hunches. After all, I'm the one it's got to please most.

I've made plenty of mistakes over the years, but I don't lose sleep over them. If I create something that is over the top, I just undo it. Plants and small objects can always be moved, and even the best gardens can be enhanced and improved. Making a good garden better is part of the fun of gardening.

I enjoy watching and working in my garden as it grows and evolves from season to season. And I enjoy the eternal dance of its elements, the pairing of its opposites, and the alchemical magic that transforms it to something that, to me, has the luster of gold.

Use parts of the garden's hardscape to enrich plant combinations. The smooth, clay vessel and the rough, gravel path play off the soft, fuzzy features of borage.

Pollarding Trees into Shrubs

I always heard that willows get big too fast and that their branches are always breaking off. People call them dirty trees. But on my wet site they're one of the few plants that really thrive. And I love their swaying branches; the bark that comes in colors of red, yellow, or green; foliage that's blue, green, or variegated; and—most of all—the wild, corkscrew curlicues of the curly willows.

I've learned to use pollarding—cutting all of a tree's main branches back to the trunk—to turn a big tree into something more akin to a shrub. It's a fair amount of work, as the willows need trimming three or four times a year. My basic technique is simple. Once the tree grows to a 4-ft. or 5-ft. height, I top it with a chain saw in late fall, then cut off any other branches until all that's left is a stick in the ground. The next spring, nubbins of new growth form at the top and give birth to new branches. I give them a little time to develop before cutting off all but the most interesting three or five new branches, making sure they are evenly spaced so the tree won't look lopsided. Then I let them grow, pruning them back when they threaten to get too large or too bushy with twiggy growth. The result is almost like bonsai—something that looks like a full-sized tree grows in a small-sized space.

JIM YORK

has been gardening for over 30 years. He indulges his passion for pruning on his own 2½-acre garden in Newtown, Connecticut.

Sculpting
Trees *and*
Shrubs

A few tools and a little imagination can turn woody plants into works of art. Here, a willow has been pollarded into a shrubby tree form and a rose of Sharon has been bundled into an arch.

MY FIRST PAINTING was also my last. I have always seen pictures in my mind's eye, so I figured it couldn't be too hard to capture my visions on canvas or paper. I enrolled in art school and, soon enough, set brush to canvas. The murky-looking result was so bad that I decided I'd be better off drawing. I wasn't any good at that either. Frustrated, I left art school but stayed close to art, and eventually opened a small gallery in Manhattan. But it wasn't until I started gardening that I discovered my true artistic calling.

As it turns out, I'm a sculptor, and my medium is trees. In 30 years of pursuing arboreal art, I've used everything from stones to saws in my efforts to transform woody plants into all kinds of wondrous shapes. I've turned shrubs into vines, pollarded willows to wild effect, and bundled the branches of a rose of Sharon to create a colorful garden archway. There's nothing orthodox about my

Turn Pine Branches into Clouds

I bought some Japanese black pines as small, foot-long whips for less than $2 each. Ten years later, they started to take shape, and I went to work, lopping off a branch here and trimming back there. I focused my efforts on sculpting those branches with the most interesting shapes, and worked to heighten their character. Once I was satisfied with the shape of an individual branch, my efforts changed, and I worked to create little cloudlike puffs of foliage at the tips.

For inspiration, I looked at books filled with pictures of Japanese gardens. There, I read that some Japanese gardeners prune the tree by removing a single needle at a time. My work wasn't nearly that painstaking. Once I established a pleasing shape, maintaining it was simply a matter of snapping the "candles" of new growth in half in late spring.

results, and I'm proud to say there's nothing traditional about my methods either.

When I first began gardening here at the home that I've lived in for three decades, I built a rock garden on a slope near the house and planted deciduous shrubs and lots of miniature conifers. But back then, conifers sold as miniatures often proved to be something else entirely. Lots of them started growing larger than I ever dreamed. Out came the pruning shears. To prevent the ever-expanding evergreens from ruining the scale of my garden, I started clipping and pruning, nicking off this branch and that. I liked the results and, in time, I became much more bold. I started whacking off big limbs, directing a tree to grow this way or that, and even, on occasion, removing enough branches to create a "window" so I could see through at least part of a tree to get a glimpse of the garden beyond. I taught myself all I know about pruning, and though I've killed a lot of plants in the process, experience has proven a good teacher.

PRUNE WHENEVER INSPIRATION STRIKES

Here are few of what I consider the basics of pruning. First, there's the issue of when to prune. I had always been told to prune in early spring, so I did that for years. Then I realized you can't plan for the way a tree will look when it's leafed out. Now I do a lot of my pruning in late spring or even summer, when trees are in full leaf. Unless it's a flowering plant—in which case I try to prune as soon as possible after it's finished blossoming—I prune whenever inspiration strikes, no matter what the season.

Neatness is important to me, and I hate looking at the bumpy nubs left by carelessly pruned branches, so I cut as close to the branch or trunk as I can. Sometimes, I use my fingers to rub off tiny branches or leaves. I try not to worry too much about trees that are bleeders (those that ooze a lot of sap after being cut), but I do prune gradually, and never remove more than a quarter of a tree or shrub at a time. Pruning is a gradual art, and there are trees in my yard, like a Japanese maple and a weeping hemlock, that I've been working on for decades.

Then, of course, there's the question of what to prune. This can be the tough one, because there's no going back once you make a cut. To me, it's a matter of what one of our former presidents called "the vision thing." Martin Eddison, my gardening pal Sydney's husband, put it this way when asked how he carved a bear out of block of wood. First, Martin said, you have to look at the block of wood until you see a bear in it. Then, you simply cut everything else away. I do the same thing, more or less, with plants.

Prune Japanese Maples for Shape

I've always admired the art of bonsai, and seeing what its devotees could do with Japanese maples made me a passionate fan of those lovely trees. I now have more than 20, including over a dozen different cultivars. I love pruning them. All the experts said to prune in early spring, but I couldn't tell how the tree would look when it leafed out, so to get a better feel for what I was doing, I did most of my pruning when the tree was covered with foliage. The plant never showed any ill effects, and the lessons I learned were so effective that now I do prune when the tree is bare.

My rules are simple: Cut anything growing downward and any branches that cross with another. The results please me visually and encourage vigorous growth on top of the tree—the more you remove from the bottom, the more the tree grows on top. I also cut to enhance the overall design of a tree, but that's more interpretive. Sometimes I just grab a cluster of branches and lop off the tips all at once, just as if I were giving it a haircut. To me, that's a nice way to layer the plant.

Girdle Sprawling Plants

I wanted something spiky and Italianate in the garden, like the cypress spires I've seen. Eventually, I planted an Irish juniper, but saw that it got too bushy. Then I thought wrapping it with fishing line might give the desired effect. I coiled some sturdy 20-lb. test line tightly around the tree until it looked like a tenderloin ready for the oven. By the next year, new growth hid the line and the tree looked great. I later learned that many junipers at the English garden of Sissinghurst were girdled just like mine. I've used the same technique with rose of Sharon to create tight, geometrically shaped bundles of bloom.

"A lot of my favorite specimens were once overgrown monstrosities that I've salvaged with pruning shears"

Make Weeping Woodies Grow Upright

Some of the most beautiful weeping trees and shrubs are so sprawling they look more like a ground cover than anything else—unless they get a little help at standing upright. This Chinese dogwood wanted to flop, so I tied its main leader to a stake to encourage it to grow upright. To get the droopy branches to grow upwards, I built little goalpost-like supports out of bamboo and used them to prop up the branches. With the supports helping to form the tree's framework, all that was left for me was to prune away some smaller branches and side shoots in order to clean up and enhance the structure.

Of course, I'm not carving bears. Instead, I emulate what most people would think of as a Japanese style, and strive for an artfully natural, gracefully flowing look that's pleasing to the eye.

CREATE ARTFUL SHAPES

The first thing I look for in a tree or shrub is character. Whether I'm at the nursery buying something new or in the garden contemplating a more mature specimen, I look closely at the shape of a plant's trunk and the arrangement of its branches. Eventually, a pattern will emerge, or at least the suggestion of a pattern. If I don't see anything, I can't cut. Basically I try to create structural form from the chaos of branches and twigs, bringing order to the wilderness as it were. I think of it as refining nature. Creating a sense of line is what my work is all about.

Sometimes, it's best to let a woody plant grow for a few years before starting to prune.

A lot depends on the type of plant. I start pruning Japanese maples as soon as I get them home, but might wait years to trim a conifer.

I enjoy surveying my trees and shrubs, and often evaluate them from different parts of the garden or from a picnic area in the middle of it all. I've planted lots of trees and shrubs over the years and it's become routine to discover things that have outgrown the scale of the garden and need attention. A lot of my favorite specimens were once overgrown monstrosities that I've salvaged with pruning shears and, in extreme cases, a chain saw. Now, I love to look for challenges. Sometimes I think that pruning has taken over my soul.

Limb Up Shrubs into Tree Form

To me, the most interesting woody plants are often shrubs rather than trees. I love this shrubby weeping hemlock, but I wanted a tree, not a shrub, in this spot. So, after the hemlock got some size, I began pruning off its lower branches to expose the trunks and make its droopy branches seem to soar. To me, it now looks like a tree. I've used this technique on other shrubs, and although the rule says to prune only after flowering, I cut back branches whenever the mood strikes. It's best to do this gradually, over a couple of years. I've accidentally killed a lot of plants, but I've also created some wonderful surprises, such as making what I call butterflies—single trees with two big wings of foliage—by cutting branches out of the middle of a shrub. Doing this radical pruning makes me fully involved in the moment—it's almost like Zen.

WORKING *with* COLOR

2

THE FIRST THING THAT ATTRACTS most people to gardening is brightly colored flowers. And our first gardens are often a riot of color. Once we get this out of our system, we can begin to design with color more effectively. We can apply the principles of color harmonies and contrasts. We can choose color combinations to create moods—whether it's the joyful mood of bright reds and oranges or the more soothing mood of pastels. We'll learn which colors recede into the distance, which appear to bring the garden closer to touch, and which are considered "peacekeepers" in a garden of many colors.

Just as important, we'll learn to think about color beyond flowers. We'll discover the sometimes subtle, yet often dramatic differences in foliage colors; how to think of color in different seasons; and how to combine flower color with other colors in the garden—the paint on our house, paving materials, and garden accents like containers or sculpture.

SYDNEY EDDISON

teaches gardening at the New York Botanical Garden. The author of four gardening books, including *The Self-Taught Gardener*, she writes and lectures widely.

A Painterly Approach to Planting

The colors of sun and fire like reds, oranges, and yellows seem to leap toward the viewer. Hot color harmonies lend themselves well to both stimulating landscapes and vibrant paintings.

ROBERT FULGHUM LEARNED all he needed to know in kindergarten. I learned most of life's important lessons between the ages of 6 and 10 at The Country Day School in Watertown, Connecticut. It was a wonderful place where students painted pictures and built houses out of crates. We sang, danced, and wrote plays, stories, and poems. I became a writer thanks to that school, and it was there that I also learned about color. Seeds planted all those years ago grew into a lifelong fascination with the subject. It took the form of painting in oils and watercolors during my teens and found an even more satisfactory outlet, a decade later, in gardening.

REFRACTED SUNLIGHT GAVE RISE TO THE COLOR WHEEL

As you may recall from your own school days, Isaac Newton established that sunlight contains all the colors of the rainbow. He intercepted beams of sunlight with a glass prism, which split the white light into bands of its respective colors: red, orange, yellow, green, blue, and violet. He described these colors collectively as the solar spectrum.

Based on Newton's 1666 discovery, the color wheel was contrived by Moses Harris in the 18th century. To illustrate relationships among colors, Newton had sketched out a circular black and white diagram. Harris reproduced the figure using pigments and divided it like a pie into wedges of red, orange, yellow, green, blue, and violet.

Think of the color wheel as the face of a clock. The three primary colors, so called because all other colors can be made from them, are equally spaced from each other: red at twelve o'clock; yellow at four o'clock; and blue at eight o'clock. In between are the secondary colors: orange, a combination of red and yellow; green, a combination of blue and yellow; and violet, made by mixing red and blue.

On either side of the primary colors are intermediate colors, which are made by combining primary and secondary colors. Flanking red, you have red-violet to the left and red-orange to the right. Yellow is sandwiched in between yellow-orange and yellow-green, and so on. The colors of sun and fire, and their in-between shades, are warm colors. Their emotional impact is stimulating, and they seem to advance toward you. Cool colors—sky blue, blue-violet, and sea green—have the opposite effect. They retreat into the distance, producing an atmosphere of calm and a sense of space.

However, the qualities of both warm and cool colors can be altered. Chartreuse, made by adding green to yellow, can be considered a warm shade of green or a cool shade of yellow. Likewise, red-violet could be a cool red or a warm violet.

To complete your color vocabulary there are also tints and tones. A tint is a color with white added—pink is a tint of red. Tones are made by adding black to any pure hue. "Hue" is a synonym for color and is used interchangeably in this chapter.

USE ADJACENT COLORS
TO CREATE HARMONY

When I first started gardening, I didn't care what color the flowers were as long as they bloomed together. Daylilies, being tough and

adaptable, were among my first successes. And because their principal colors ran to shades of yellow, orange, and red, I found myself drawn to the warm side of the spectrum. While there is something immensely cheering about these colors, creating a "hot" garden was not a conscious decision. It was the nature of the

(OPPOSITE AND ABOVE) Cool colors recede into the distance. Soothing shades of blues, greens, and whites compose a peaceful setting.

"Harmony in this sense has more to do with relationships than with absence of discord."

three adjacent colors. Red is on one side of orange, yellow on the other, and orange itself contains both red and yellow. The rule is that from three to six adjacent colors having one color in common results in harmony.

PAIR OPPOSITE COLORS FOR LIVELY CONTRAST

Contrast is the other basic technique for using color. While harmony depends on likeness and sharing, contrast is about differences. For the liveliest contrast, juxtapose colors from opposite sides of the color wheel, such as red and green, blue and orange, yellow and violet. These are called complementary colors. Having no common pigment and being exact opposites, they intensify each other by their differences. For dramatic effect, nothing beats pairing complementary colors.

Examples of paired complements abound. Easter wouldn't be Easter without foil-wrapped, yellow and purple eggs. Nor is nature timid about complementary color schemes. Think of flame-colored foliage against the fierce blue of an October sky.

Refer to the color wheel illustration to see the relationship between these colors, or better still, buy a color wheel of your own. They are available for about $5 at art supply stores. Once you own a color wheel and begin to think about contrast and harmony, you'll see how common these techniques are in nature and in everyday life.

WHITE STEALS THE SHOW, SO USE IT WISELY

Nothing rivals white for power and brilliance. White is the most reflective of all colors, putting the brightest reds and sunniest yellows in the shade. White demands attention. Years ago, I had several clumps of white phlox in the

daylilies, and I simply went with the flow. However, there is a reason the combination of yellow, red, and orange worked. It is a color harmony, which is one of the two most basic ways to use color effectively.

Harmony in this sense has more to do with relationships than with absence of discord. In music, it describes a relationship between notes. In terms of color, it describes the physical relation of colors to one another as they are fitted together to form either the rainbow or the man-made color wheel.

As luck and the daylilies would have it, my summer display at that time was based on

The color wheel mimics the face of a clock. Opposite colors such as red and green contrast; adjacent colors are harmonious.

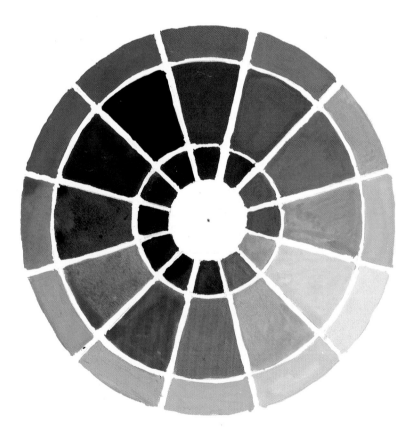

perennial border. The massive, conical heads were beautiful in themselves but devastating to the neighboring daylilies. From a distance, the border looked like an unfinished painting with great patches of white canvas showing through.

White is a wonderful color, but must be used wisely in small amounts. An all-white garden can be a dream of loveliness. A flurry of small white flowers can clean up murky colors and bring freshness to a planting. The amount and the quality of white are what matters. Creamy white is less reflective than sheet white and might blend in with tints of yellow, pink, and blue. Icy white can be the key for a ravishing cool scheme of blue, blue-violet, white, silver, and green. White is a superb foil for orange, which somehow holds its own against the glare.

GREEN KEEPS THE PEACE, GRAY BLENDS COLORS

No matter what colors you put together, nature has seen to it that green will predominate. Green is the easiest color on the human eye. It is also the peacekeeper among warring colors. It enhances cool colors and takes the edge off hot colors. With enough green foliage in a flower bed, anything goes.

If white is the prima donna and green the peacemaker, gray is the great blender. There are many plants that provide gray leaves to combine with flowers. But gray, too, has many shades and moods. A bright silver-gray can be almost as disruptive as white itself. However, it can also be used to stunning effect in contrast to somber foliage plants, such as dark-red perilla (*Perilla frutescens*) and rich purple smokebush (*Cotinus coggyria*).

As a blender, particularly with pastels, look for gray-greens, blue-grays, and shades of

pewter gray or steel-blue gray. Gray also creates unity as an edging. In my garden, a ribbon of gray lamb's ears binds the colors in the border into a whole.

My *Chambers 20th-Century Dictionary* defines color as a "sensation in the eye induced by electromagnetic waves of different frequencies in the presence of light." If I had known that at the age of 10, I doubt I would have become hooked on the subject for life. Fortunately, The Country Day School believed in hands-on learning, and I became intrigued with colors and the color wheel. Of course, light shining through tissue-thin flower petals and flickering across wind-stirred leaves provides a palette that makes color wheels seem like crude devices. That's why playing with color in the garden is even more entrancing than using pigments on canvas.

Use gray as a blender. Muted shades and tints of gray such as blue-gray and pewter-gray are particularly effective with pastels.

ELISABETH SHELDON

is author of *A Proper Garden* and *The Flamboyant Garden*. She is a frequent garden lecturer and previously ran a small nursery specializing in perennials and herbs.

A Home for Hot Colors

In the author's enclosed garden, hot-colored flowers in vivid reds, oranges and yellows freely co-mingle.

FOR MANY YEARS I have tended a long mixed border consisting mostly of perennials. Its pastels of pink, lavender, lemon yellow, blue, gray and white, punctuated with an occasional touch of crimson, reflect the dominant colors of the perennial flowers that survive in my New York State garden in USDA Hardiness Zone 5. They are cool colors, peaceful and serene. At times I tried to include hot colors—strong, brassy yellows, oranges, scarlets or vermilions—but I found they disturbed the harmony of the border. I thus banished the deep yellow yarrows, black-eyed Susans, false sunflowers and other strident individuals to the far reaches of my temporary beds. I didn't throw them on the compost heap, you will notice; I merely isolated the hot-colored flowers, keeping them until I would find a way to use them effectively. Meanwhile I trotted out to visit them occasionally when I needed a pick-me-up.

The orange 'Mandarin' calendula is backed by the yellow-centered 'Little Red Riding Hood' dahlia and golden yarrow, with a dollop of purple 'Victoria' salvia for contrast. Hot-colored flowers make a garden jump to life.

Now I have loved (and still love) my long, pastel border, but with the passage of years I began to long for stronger stuff. I began to think of ways to use intense colors where they wouldn't interfere with the cool border symphony. I considered several sites before I finally decided to enclose part of my old plant nursery, at one end of the pastel border and adjacent to my woods garden, and make it into a garden of hot colors. It was a particularly good spot for the new garden, because visitors would walk along the long, cool border, then suddenly be knocked flat when they encountered the explosion of color.

The border and new garden look very different. My informal perennial border of pastels is designed with a series of curves on the front edge played against a long, straight line behind. Since the new garden would be inside a smallish rectangular area (about 20 ft. by 30 ft.), I felt it required a formal plan with no curves. A narrow central path begins at the gate, bisects three paved rectangles and ends with a bench. It's a very stiff and formal outline, compensated for by the exuberance of the planting.

It would have been nice to enclose the garden with a tall, clipped hedge, but the space was too small. Nor did I want to wait for shrubs to grow or to spend a lot of time shearing them. I thus opted for a plain, 5-ft.-tall cedar fence. By the time the fence was up and I had laid the paving and planted the garden, I had a secret jungle retreat. And there I go, at least once a day, to sit, to drink in the color combinations and to bring myself to a mild state of innocent intoxication.

DESIGN PRINCIPLES FOR HOT-COLORED FLOWERS

In designing and planting this garden, I have developed four principles that can be applied to other bold gardens.

In fall, the flowers of *Helenium* 'Bruno', a perennial, blanket 2-ft.- to 4-ft.-tall stems.

First, because hot colors are so visually stimulating (and hard to combine with other colors), I think they should be separated from the rest of the garden. Besides, if you look at them every time you walk outdoors, they're apt to lose their impact. Because the area I chose for my hot-color garden is so flat, I had to enclose it to keep it distinct. Gardeners with more uneven territory could separate hot colors by putting them on one side of a knoll or terrace. Or they could place them in back of a hedge or on the far side of a building.

Second, choose complementary building materials. A building or fence behind the planting should be of a color that will enhance the flower colors, not detract from them. The gray of cedar fencing seems perfect, but white could be even more dramatic. Brown wood might be harmonious, but would create a heavier effect than gray or white. Avoid by all means pink, red, yellow or bright green backgrounds. (The green of a hedge, which can serve as a perfectly suitable backdrop, is quite

> *"Because hot colors are so visually stimulating, I think they should be separated from the rest of the garden."*

Flame red 'Vesuvius' campion sizzles for several weeks in summer next to 'Marmalade' black-eyed Susan.

different from most greens that come out of a can.) Pink, red or yellow would cause flowers of related colors to lose importance. For the paving, the gray-maroon of paving bricks, which I used, is generally harmonious. Weathered brick would also work well. Gray flagstone would have been a fine color, but hard to fit into the small, geometric shapes of my paved area.

Third, repeat colors and shapes. When I planned the planting, I remembered that in gardening as in painting, repetition of color

Orange Mexican sunflower and golden yarrow tower over reddish-orange cosmos, yellow coreopsis and red dahlias in the author's garden.

and form is absolutely necessary for harmony and unity. You don't have to use the same plant over and over, but you should find plants of the same shape and/or flower color that bloom at the same time. For example, the orange of calendulas (*Calendula officinalis* cvs.) is repeated by marigolds (*Tagetes* cvs.). Red and gold blanket flowers (*Gaillardia* spp.) echo the reds and golds of dahlias (*Dahlia* cvs.). The color repeats, although the plants do not.

I first thought of making symmetrical plantings in the new formal garden, one side as a mirror image of the other. That seemed so boring that I decided, instead, to try to balance the two sides using similar colors and forms. Tall red and gold sneezeweeds (*Helenium autumnale* cvs.) grow on both sides of the garden but are not necessarily opposite one another. *Dahlia* 'Bishop of Llandaff' stands against one fence, *Dahlia* 'Tasagore' against the other. Both have the most beautiful purple foliage and what British plantsman Graham Stuart Thomas calls "fierce" red flowers. I placed different varieties of red daylilies on each side.

Some plantings are symmetrical, though. Yellow tickseed (*Coreopsis auriculata* 'Nana'), 1 ft. tall, sits on each of the four inside corners of the garden walk. Orange lilies (*Lilium* 'Enchantment') stand with dark purple Japanese iris (*Iris ensata*) in the two far corners. Short 'Disco Red' marigolds edge opposite sides of the paths; I've paired 'Disco Orange' marigolds similarly. They hold their jewel-like, flat, single flowers tight against low, dark green, incised foliage and seem to never stop flowering. These are the only examples of perfect symmetry.

And finally, be bold. Choosing flowers for a hot-color garden involves a certain amount of experimentation and a willingness—at least in my case—to discard a few long-cherished prejudices. In our climate, a gardener has to go tropical and look for annuals and bulb plants to get a volcanic display. But I have always despised marigolds, cannas, dahlias and gladioluses. Going in for "proper" perennials as I did, I was above such frivolous individuals. For my sins, I'm now having to recant as I glory in their startling colors.

The true orange of 'Enchantment' lilies, an unusual color for a hardy perennial, appears even more vibrant paired with the purple spikes of *Salvia* 'Victoria'.

FAVORITE HOT-COLORED FLOWERS

I began my new garden with hot-colored perennials I already had in reserve: yarrows (*Achillea filipendulina* 'Gold Plate' and *A.* 'Coronation Gold') and red and yellow sneezeweeds. I also planted two tall sunflower relatives with double yellow poufs for flowers—*Heliopsis helianthoides* var. *scabra* 'Goldgefinger' and 'Goldgruwherz', which proved too big, and which I later evicted—adding red and purple bee balms (*Monarda didyma* cvs.), yellow tickseed, and red and yellow daylilies.

Then I started plowing through catalogs looking for more hot-colored flowers. I've made some wonderful discoveries. The tender perennial campion (*Lychnis* × *arkwrightii* 'Vesuvius') provides one of the most intense flame reds available, on 18-in. plants distinguished by rich maroon foliage. It blooms for several weeks and is kind enough to seed itself about every year.

Breeders have doubled the number of flower petals of the annual blanket flower (*Gaillardia pulchella* 'Red Plume'), to the point where it no longer looks like a *Gaillardia*—a procedure for which I am on record as vigorously opposing. But, since it produces an endless supply of chianti-red flowers on 1½-ft.-tall plants, I must shamefacedly admit to being grateful for it. I use the perennial *Gaillardia* × *grandiflora* 'Burgunder' with no shame, since it has a single row of deep red petals.

For me, dark purple—either the true purple of some flowers or the "purple" (actually dark wine, maroon or blackish red) of leaves—is the best companion to the warmer hues. Along with the 'Bishop of Llandaff' and 'Tasagore' dahlias, I've planted 'Japanese Bishop', all for their purple foliage. Their leaves echo those of shiso (*Perilla frutescens*) and basil (*Ocimum basilicum* 'Purple Ruffles'). Both are easy-to-grow annuals that I've planted throughout the garden. Shiso loses its lovely color when it goes to seed and must be discarded, but 'Purple Ruffles' basil remains attractive all summer. The tender sweet-potato vine (*Ipomoea batatas* 'Blackie') has the darkest foliage of all, with near-black, deeply lobed leaves.

My garden is full of red, yellow and orange, especially in July. *Cosmos bipinnatus* 'Sunny Red', an annual, isn't really red but a pretty reddish-orange. It blooms for several weeks.

"Repetition of color and form is absolutely necessary for harmony and unity."

The dark red blossoms of the annual 'Red Plume' blanket flower cap 1½-ft.-tall plants all summer. Annuals can provide bolder colors and longer bloom times than most perennials can.

Pure orange is found in 'Mandarin' calendulas, in some of the daylilies and especially in 'Enchantment' lilies. The 4-ft. Mexican sunflower (*Tithonia rotundifolia*), an annual, has velvety leaves and large, soft orange (another orange!) daisies. It shows well against the big purple flowers of *Clematis* 'Jackmanii' on the fence. There is also an orange-gold swath of the annual black-eyed Susan (*Rudbeckia hirta* 'Marmalade'), bold and brassy. Both it and the Mexican sunflower seem to bloom forever.

When purple Japanese iris fade, they are followed by the purple spikes of annual salvia (*Salvia farinacea* 'Victoria'). Short, fat mounds of 'Little Red Riding Hood' dahlia have single red flowers with yellow centers, set off by purple bee balms and 15-in.-tall blue spikes of veronica (*Veronica spicata* 'Blaufuchs'). There's lots of gold yarrow, lots of red and yellow daylilies and behind them, proper lilies (*Lilium* 'Gran Paradiso' and 'Barcelona'). They make outfacing cartwheels of orange, scarlet and dark red.

Thread-leaved coreopsis (*Coreopsis verticillata* 'Zagreb') is pretty with its sheets of small, yellow ray flowers and feathery foliage. Not smashing but nice. More striking are the blossoms, deep yellow and brown, of the annual chrysanthemum (*Chrysanthemum carinatum*). The vermilion knobs of globe amaranth (*Gomphrena* 'Strawberry Fields'),bloom on eternally through summer and fall until a hard frost. These flowers never seem to fade, flop or drop. Apparently they're as everlasting in life as in death.

You may have been appalled by this account, or you may have been inspired to plant your own garden of hot colors. If so, you'll have to search for plants that will thrive in your environment. If you garden in the South or on the West Coast, you might have the advantage in this regard—the growing season is longer, and you needn't lift so many bulbs and tubers for overwintering indoors. The combination of heat and humidity in the South, however, might rule out some plants I can grow here in New York.

When you've chosen your plants, you can begin to combine them in ways that suit you. You may want to include bright pinks or temper the atmosphere with whites or blues or silver instead of the dark purple flowers or foliage I prefer, but that's only personal taste. Last summer I thought to rest the eye with grays and whites as well as purples. I tried gray, felt-leaved licorice plant (*Helichrysum petiolore*), which is not hardy here, in pots. I also planted a dusty miller (*Senecio cineraria*) against the back wall. This striking perennial bears bright silver, finely cut foliage. I think the licorice plants were a mistake—they looked irrelevant or as if they were all dressed up and had come to the wrong party. But there are so many other possibilities. Are you intrigued? Then I encourage you to get out the catalogues and start planning.

The regal purple of the clematis on the fence and of the iris in the foreground is a foil for the brassy gold of a long-blooming, annual black-eyed Susan. Hot colors like these wake up any garden visitor.

MARIETTA O'BYRNE

and her husband, Ernie, own Northwest Garden Nursery in Eugene, Oregon, which specializes in perennials. Marietta lectures and teaches on various areas of gardening.

Design for Drama

with Colorful Foliage

Dynamic foliage combinations provide a long season of interest. This pairing of *Canna* 'Pretoria' and *Dahlia* 'Bishop of Llandaff' looks good all season long.

M Y GARDEN IS MUCH MORE than a pretty decoration around the house. To me, it is a creation with a life of its own, a dynamo brimming with vitality. And it freely shares that energy with me, just as a good painting invigorates a viewer.

I've learned that almost nothing in the garden has a more lively presence than foliage. Even when there's nothing in bloom, it can provide sculptural shape, intriguing texture, and most important, color. I think intriguing combinations of colorful foliage can be just as rewarding as more fleeting combinations with colorful flowers. And for power-packed garden compositions that really fire things up, it's hard to beat mixes based on purple and gold foliage. These colors make a strong impact and I love using them, albeit with a certain amount of discretion.

Gold foliage always attracts attention because of its brightness and warmth. But it is best used in moderation, to create highlights throughout the garden.

PAIR PURPLE AND GOLD FOLIAGE FOR VISUAL EXCITEMENT

Garden writer John Kelly says, "Do not allow yourself to believe that yellow and purple leaves belong together. They are as compatible as Cain and Abel."

Well, I beg to differ. Yellow and purple are complementary colors, which means they are on opposite sides of the color wheel, a pairing that produces the greatest contrast. At the same time, the two colors enhance each other—each becomes more intense to the eye than if they were placed singly. That's exactly the effect I want. To me, there's real visual excitement in almost any pairing of these two bold colors, especially on the scale provided by small trees or large shrubs. One of my favorite pairings is a large gold-leaved elderberry (*Sambucus racemosa* 'Plumosa Aurea') serving as a backdrop for the purple mound made by a pollarded smoke tree (*Cotinus coggygria* 'Royal Purple'). This twosome looks good from spring to fall.

The key to tasteful pairings with purple and gold is moderation. Combinations with such strong impact cease to draw the eye if repeated too often. When that happens, we suffer from visual overload or simply deem it tasteless. With this combination, less is more.

BOLD COLORS WORK BEST WITH A BACKDROP OF GREEN

Another secret for using these daring foliage colors—by themselves or in combination with each other—is planting them in a setting rich with plenty of healthy, deep-green foliage. The green creates a peaceful resting place for the eye and allows it to pause between onslaughts of vibrant colors. To keep the green foliage looking lush and abundant, it's vitally important to keep up the fertility of soil. To maintain that lush look, my husband, Ernie, and I have found nothing beats using plenty of good, organic mulch. We pile loads and loads of rich compost on our garden beds every winter.

If the green is to come from the foliage of perennials, you might take to heart our own credo for success in the garden: "Divide and

"I think intriguing combinations of colorful foliage can be just as rewarding as more fleeting combinations with colorful flowers."

Gold-needled conifers provide year-round interest, and their crisp, richly textured look helps perk up the garden in late summer.

Purple is actually a catch-all expression for a whole range of color, most typically a mix of red and blue which is often enhanced by overtones of bronze-brown or black. Many gardeners refer to the same range of color as black. Whatever you call it, these somber colors absorb light and seem to recede into the background. Their true glory is revealed only in the company of other colors.

Gold, on the other hand, is the great brightener. Like purple, it too encompasses a mix of colors, ranging from acid-green chartreuse to soft, buttery yellow to gold. All these colors are close to yellow, the primary color that reflects the most light, so they appear much brighter to our eye than reds or blues. The sun looks yellow too, which accounts, at least in part, for the psychologically cheering effect we associate with that color. It also contributes to our perception of yellow as a warm color. I like using garden golds to bring light to shady areas.

PLAN A PLANTING AROUND PURPLE

Because it needs the color of companion plants to bring it to life, purple can be an effective anchor for a planting scheme. Since almost any other color works well with purple, it's hard to go wrong no matter what you plant. I've used a canna with huge reddish-purple leaves, *Canna* 'Wyoming', as a centerpiece in a bed of hot reds, greens, and golds. The somber depths of the canna's color are intensified by the reds, which seem to glow more deeply as a result of their pairing with purple. Plants such as black-leaved, red-flowered dahlias (*Dahlia* 'Bishop of Llandaff'), yellow and orange lilies, euphorbias, and the yellow, green-striped *Canna* 'Pretoria' also find

Trees and shrubs with colored foliage add color on a grand scale. A smokebush and a golden elderberry brighten the garden.

Mulch." In addition to the benefits of mulching with compost, we've found that dividing perennials often keeps them growing vigorously.

EACH COLOR HAS ITS OWN ROLE IN DESIGN

Though the combination of purple and gold is dynamic, each color is strong enough by itself to play a specific role in creating dynamic effects in the garden.

a home here. This combo has the intensity of a brush fire.

Since purple itself consists of colors from the hot (red) and cool (blue) side of the spectrum, it also serves as a buffer between colors that would normally clash. Some people refer to it as the peacemaking color. I often use one of my favorite purple perennials—*Cryptotaenia japonica* f. *atropurpurea*, a totally wonderful and underused, rusty-black foliage plant—as a referee between colors I wouldn't normally place next to each other, like pink and yellow.

USE GOLD AS A BEACON

When I think of yellow foliage, I think of a sick plant. But, if instead I call it golden foliage, I envision a plant glowing with health. Such is the power of words. But whether you call it yellow or gold, this color always attracts attention. Because of its brightness and the feeling of warmth it suggests, too much yellow foliage can overpower a planting scheme. I

Green creates a peaceful resting place for the eye. Use plenty of rich green foliage to provide a foil for more vibrant colors.

"Because of its brightness, too much yellow foliage can overpower a planting scheme."

Gold and purple enhance each other. In combination, each color becomes more intense to the eye.

limit my use of it to creating highlights throughout the garden.

Gold is at its best when used to brighten the shade. Placed at the edge of a shady path, the color is like a beacon, beckoning you onward. Gold used in the shade is like a bit of sunshine come to ground and the effect is more real if, like a dancing ray of sun, there is movement and pattern to the foliage as well. Take for example a bed of gold and gold-variegated hostas. There is color, but the effect is rather stodgy. Edge it with weeping Japanese fountain grass (*Hakonechloa macra* 'Aureola'), or plant green ferns or golden tufted sedge (*Carex elata* 'Knightshayes') in between, and it comes alive with every puff of wind, mimicking the effect of sunlight even on cloudy days.

Using gold foliage is more challenging in sunny spots because direct sunlight can scorch the leaves of some gold-foliaged plants in high summer. So, in sunny spots, whenever a touch of gold is called for to brighten an area or contrast with darker foliage, I'm careful to use gold-leaved plants that tolerate sun, like golden dogwood (*Cornus* alba 'Aurea') or golden feverfew (*Tanacetum parthenium* 'Aureum'). It takes a bit of trial-and-error testing, depending on the sun's power in your area. Sometimes I try new plants only to find the sun burns their foliage by late summer, but a great effect in spring may be worth the price of a slightly burnt look in August.

For a more substantial effect, there are gold-needled conifers that will thrive in sun and shade. They give the garden winter interest and provide a texture that I feel is often lacking. Their neat, crisp appearance keeps a leafy planting looking fresh, and helps prevent the mushy, overgrown look that can overtake the garden in late summer and fall.

It pays to be a bit adventurous and take a risk with color schemes in your garden. Remember, if you don't like a plant where it is, you can always move it. So, if your garden recedes into too much good taste and timidity, try some brassy golds and purples. Their energy can be a refreshing and vital part of the garden.

Enliven plantings with golden grasses that dance in the wind. Gold-tufted sedge sparkles in a bed of hostas.

A Foliage Fancier's Guide to the Best of Purple and Gold

FAVORITES FOR PURPLE FOLIAGE

Trees and Shrubs
Purple smoke tree (*Cotinus coggygria* 'Royal Purple')
'Albury Purple' tutsan (*Hypericum androsaemum* 'Albury Purple')
Purple-leaved elderberry (*Sambucus nigra* 'Purpurea' or 'Guincho Purple')
Black twig dogwood (*Cornus alba* 'Kesselringii')
Purple-leaved filbert (*Corylus maxima* 'Purpurea')

Perennials
Cow parsley (*Anthriscus sylvestris* 'Ravenswing')
Snakeroot (*Cimicifuga simplex* 'Brunette' or 'Hillside Black Beauty')
Black mondo grass (*Ophiopogon planiscapus* 'Nigrescens')
Cryptotaenia japonica f. *atropurpurea*
Wood spurge (*Euphorbia amygdaloides* 'Purpurea')
Purple spurge (*Euphorbia dulcis* 'Chameleon')
Red switch grass (*Panicum virgatum* 'Rehbraun')
Japanese blood grass (*Imperata cylindrica* 'Rubra')

Annuals and Tender Perennials
Dahlia 'Bishop of Llandaff'
Canna 'Wyoming'
Black-leaved pepper (*Capsicum annuum* 'Black Prince')
Black-leaved sweet potato (*Ipomoea batatas* 'Blackie')

GOLD-LEAVED PLANTS THAT GLOW

Trees and Shrubs
Dwarf golden Hinoki cypress (*Chamaecyparis obtusa* 'Nana Lutea')
Golden dogwood (*Cornus alba* 'Aurea')
Gold-leaved tall tutsan (*Hypericum* × *inodorum* 'Summergold')
Virginia pine (*Pinus virginiana* 'Wate's Golden')
Golden elderberry (*Sambucus racemosa* 'Plumosa Aurea')
Golden Japanese spirea (*Spiraea japonica* 'Lime Mound')
Golden Japanese yew (*Taxus cuspidata* 'Gold Queen')
Golden white cedar (*Thuja occidentalis* 'Rheingold')

Perennials
Libertia peregrinans 'Bronze Sword'
Golden feverfew (*Tanacetum parthenium* 'Aureum')
Smyrnium perfoliatum
Japanese fountain grass (*Hakonechloa macra* 'Aureola')
Golden tufted sedge (*Carex elata* 'Knightshayes' and 'Aurea')
Hosta 'Sun Power', 'Chinese Sunrise', and 'Sum and Substance'
Golden deadnettle (*Lamium maculatum* 'Aureum')
Golden creeping Jenny (*Lysimachia nummularia* 'Aurea')

Annuals and Tender Perennials
Canna 'Pretoria'
Helichrysum petiolare 'Limelight'
Gold-leaved geraniums (*Pelargonium* cvs.)
Gold-leaved sweet potato (*Ipomoea batatas* 'Marguerite')

Coloring *the* Garden

KEEYLA MEADOWS

is the owner of Keeyla Meadows Gardens and Art. She is a garden designer, painter, sculptor, potter, and photographer who is noted for her distinctive use of color.

A brilliant color scheme: Keeyla Meadows accents her house with bright, contrasting garden colors including pink roses and lilies, blue baboon flowers (*Babiana* spp.) and yellow *Tagetes lemmonii*.

I AM AN ARTIST who works in many media, and I am also a garden designer. Learning to create three-dimensional shapes through sculpture gave me a foundation for my garden. But it was studying plants, not art, that introduced me to the delights of using color.

Painting with foliage and flower colors in my Albany, California, garden (USDA Hardiness Zone 9) has since bloomed into a passion for painting on canvas. But I see my own garden as my primary blank canvas, open to an ongoing flow of artistic expression, a work of mixed media. I look for repetition, or resonance, of color when choosing plants and materials for hardscaping.

SELECTING A COLOR PALETTE

I work with color by first choosing a palette. A palette can be any combination of selected colors. Each palette has a different tone and sings a different song. I like to experi-

Pink and purple harmony: A reddish-purple, painted fence in the author's garden inspired her to plant pink- and purple-flowered lilies and hardy geraniums (*Geranium* spp.).

ment. Luckily, I have many clients' gardens where I've been able to work with new palettes.

When combining foliage and flower colors, I am guided by a sense of whimsy, inventiveness, passion and delight. Sometimes, instead of planting flowers, I like to try colorful blueberries (*Vaccinium* spp.), strawberries (*Fragaria* cvs.) or berry-producing shrubs, such as cotoneasters (*Cotoneaster* spp.) and barberries (*Berberis* spp.).

I consider the colors of the house and the bright, warm or cool quality of light in the garden when I create a palette. I also may be inspired by benches or sculptures that are in the garden.

Palettes can be harmonious or contrasting. Repeating the colors of a house produces a harmonious palette. But a garden palette that contrasts with a house's colors can produce a powerful visual effect. My garden has both.

In my front-yard garden, I have a bright, hot-colored palette that contrasts with the less intense colors of my house. There I grow marigolds (*Tagetes* cvs.) with bright yellow-orange flowers; yellow roses, such as 'Bloomfield Dainty', 'Alchymist' and 'Sunny June'; 'Garnet' penstemon (*Penstemon* 'Andenken an Friedrich Hahn'); coral- and red-flowered autumn sage (*Salvia greggii*); and rose-pink and yellow rock roses (*Cistus* × *pulverulentus* 'Sunset').

In the back garden, I have a harmonious palette. Soft pink 'The Fairy', 'Meidiland' and 'Felicia' roses blend with the pink *Dianthus* and *Salvia* species, *Diascia vigilis*, and

"Sometimes, instead of planting flowers, I try colorful blueberries (Vaccinium *spp.), strawberries* (Fragaria *cvs.) or berry-producing shrubs"*

Testing a Color Palette before Planting

When I do a painting, I start with a pencil drawing on paper; this serves as the painting's structure. Then I create a palette, choosing tubes of paint I want to use. Finally, I squeeze out the colors and paint on a canvas.

Likewise, I choose a palette of plants and test them before devoting a whole area to the colors. It's fun—an adventure really—to search nurseries for plants that fit a color scheme.

I highly recommend testing a palette before installing an entire bed or garden. Here are my three favorite ways to test plant combinations for compatible color before I actually plant them:

1 Containers are a good place to be daring with combinations of annuals or perennials. With containers, you can easily try something out and make adjustments on a small scale. I like to use neutral terra-cotta pots and colorful ceramic planters to experiment with color combinations.

2 To check the colors of larger plants, such as perennials, shrubs and trees, visit a nursery. Pick the plants you are interested in and group them right in the nursery sales yard to see what works for you.

3 Finally, for an instant preview of a floral palette, put together a bouquet of cut flowers that have the colors you are considering to put into your garden.

Garden ornaments, like this arch and a painted bench, echo flower colors.

A hot, reddish-purple wall and beds of bright flowers are cooled by blue columbines and a blue-tiled walk.

Containers and accompanying plantings carry out the color theme.

'Huntington Pink' and 'Elfin Pink' penstemons.

To produce a unifying background, use masses of any color. Plant coral- and salmon-flowered plants to add warmth to the garden and accent the browns in stems and leaves. Then float a brighter accent color on top, such as blue, red, orange, yellow or magenta, by adding specimens that flower in these colors.

UNITING THE HOUSE AND GARDEN WITH COLOR

I was inspired to paint my house in the same shades of coral, red and blue-green as in an afghan I finished making just before I moved in. The red paint soon faded to a pleasing purplish tone. For the dominant colors in my garden, I selected plants with similarly colored leaves and flowers, and warm-toned hardscaping, such as red fences and bricks. Tints of coral and pink appear in lilies (*Lilium* spp.), 'Frel' strawberries, 'Felicia' roses and coral bells (*Heuchera sanguinea*).

Deeper shades of reddish purple are provided by the vivid, saucer-sized flowers of *Clematis* 'Ernest Markham'.

The centerpiece of my backyard is an arch with a morning-glory motif I designed and had fabricated from copper. A nearby weeping crabapple (*Malus* cv.) complements the arch with its coppery leaves and deep pink flowers in spring; both bring out the arch's purple patina.

Blue wasn't part of my color scheme, and it wasn't a color I could easily blend into my warm-toned palette. But I wanted to incorporate blue flowers because they bring the sky closer to the ground; so I experimented with the color. Blue-flowered lobelia (*Lobelia erinus*) trailing over the reddish purple wall at the back of my garden leads the eye down the central path, which I made of bricks and flag-

"To produce a unifying background, use masses of any color."

stones accented with blue tiles. Then I added ceramic pots with blue accents and more blue-flowered plants, such as delphiniums (*Delphinium* cvs.) and *Salvia guaranitica*.

I made yellow tiles and set them into another path to brighten a shady area. I also added yellow foliage and flowers—yellow-leaved selections, such as lilyturf (*Liriope muscari* 'Variegata'), lime-colored *Helichrysum petiolare* 'Limelight', feverfew (*Tanacetum parthenium*), spurges (*Euphorbia* spp.) and *Weigela florida* 'Variegata'; and yellow-flowering plants, such as flowering maple (*Abutilon hybridum*), pocketbook flower (*Calceolaria* spp.) and *Doronicum orientale*.

My garden is a place where I invite plants to freely sing their song, so that the magic that my colorful palette works can be appreciated.

A harmonious combination of fruit and flowers: A container of magenta geraniums and baby-blue-eyes (*Nemophila menziesii*) is set off by a pink-flowered strawberry.

SPECIAL
PLANTINGS

3

GREAT PLANTINGS don't always feature a combination of plants. Sometimes, a single plant is used in mass to create a special effect. Or a single plant stands on its own as a focal point. Much of the basis of making effective plantings is the concept of using the right plant in the right place. Certainly that includes selecting the right cultural conditions. But it also means using plants that excel for certain purposes.

For instance, creeping plants make great ground covers. Plants that prefer dry conditions often thrive in the cracks and crevices of stone walls. And many apple and pear trees have a growth habit that is suited for training into a decorative espalier.

So we'll take a look at a few special uses for plants. This is by no means a comprehensive guide to the subject, but hopefully it will give you some creative ideas for selecting appropriate plants for special places in your landscape or using plants in unique ways.

ERICA GLASENER

is a contributing editor for *Fine Gardening* and the host of HGTV's *A Gardener's Diary*. Previously she was in charge of the educational program at the Scott Arboretum of Swarthmore College.

Covering Ground
with Creeping Plants

Great ground covers look pleasing from season to season. 'Eco-Lacquered Spider' green-and-gold boasts shiny foliage that is purplish in winter and accented by tiny yellow flowers in spring.

SOMETIMES IT SEEMS that designing a garden is like solving a complex puzzle. That's actually one of the challenges of gardening I enjoy most—finding beautiful and robust plants to suit a site. And, in areas that can be the most confounding—such as along slopes, under trees, or between crevices of rocks or stepping stones—herbaceous ground covers often fill the bill.

My favorite ground-cover plants spread quickly without aggressively taking over the way that English ivy (*Hedera helix*) does. And they look stunning with little care. A few vigorous ground covers can even withstand foot traffic or the rowdy antics of pets.

Most great ground covers are essentially creepers—they grow out rather than up. Some, such as creeping raspberry (*Rubus calycinoides*, also known as *Rubus pentalobus*), travel by sending out runners and producing rootlets wherever a leaf node or stem touches the soil. Others, like *Mazus rep-*

Golden creeping oregano shines along a pathway edge. Here it accents the purple leaves of 'Chameleon' spurge.

Ground-hugging *Mazus reptans* fills in neatly around rocks. Its tiny flowers look like miniature snapdragons.

"Most great ground covers are essentially creepers—they grow out rather than up."

tans, form rosettes of foliage with roots along their stems. They're all easy to propagate by division. None of my favorites develop woody stems or deep root systems, so they are relatively easy to curtail. If they cover too much ground, I just dig up the excess growth and either transplant it, give it away, or discard it.

SOME CREEPERS LOVE THE SUN

Golden creeping thyme (*Thymus* × *citriodorus* 'Aureus') looks dainty, but it's a tough and fast-growing ground cover. I use it to rapidly fill in gaps between stepping stones or rocks. It grows to only 2 in. or 3 in. high with tiny leaves about ¼ in. wide and long. In early summer it bears small, delicate, whitish flowers. Mostly evergreen, the foliage starts with strong golden overtones and turns greener in autumn. In winter the stems take on reddish tinges. Like other thymes, golden creeping thyme is aromatic, releasing a slight lemony scent when touched, and can be used in cooking.

Another robust creeper, golden oregano (*Origanum vulgare* 'Aureum') holds its golden hue best in colder weather. A useful culinary herb, golden oregano has tiny, rounded leaves ½ in. to 1 in. wide. Its small, lavender to purple flowers stand out above the foliage in early to late summer. Combine it with other oreganos, or plant it under lavenders (*Lavendula* spp.), rosemary (*Rosemarinus officinalis*), or Japanese bloodgrass (*Imperata cylindrica* 'Red Baron') to provide a contrasting carpet of gold.

THESE SPREADERS ARE AT HOME IN EITHER SUN OR SHADE

If you want to test a plant's toughness, try growing it in the strip between the sidewalk and the street. That's where I'm using creeping raspberry as a ground cover. So far, it's proved itself a worthy roadside warrior in my

Growing Your Favorite Ground Covers

BLUE STAR CREEPER

Botanical name: *Laurentia fluviatilis*

Range: USDA Hardiness Zones 7 to 10

Culture: Grow in moist, well-drained soil in either full sun or partial shade. Plant divisions or rooted cuttings in the spring.

CREEPING RASPBERRY

Botanical name: *Rubus calycinoides* (also known as *R. pentalobus*)

Range: Zones 7 to 9

Culture: Plant in full sun or partial shade in well-drained soil. Cut off and transplant pieces of stems where roots have formed any time in the growing season.

'ECO-LACQUERED SPIDER' GREEN-AND-GOLD

Botanical name: *Chrysogonum virginianum* 'Eco-Lacquered Spider'

Range: Zones 5 to 8

Culture: While it's happiest in dappled shade, such as along woodland edges, it will also adapt to sunnier spots if it's watered during periods of drought. Plant divisions or rooted stem cuttings in the spring. In warmer climates, you can also plant in the fall.

GOLDEN CREEPING JENNY

Botanical name: *Lysimachia nummularia* 'Aurea'

Range: Zones 4 to 8

Culture: This moisture lover also adapts to dry soil. To encourage the brightest foliage, site this prostrate perennial where it gets morning sun but is shaded during the hottest part of the day. Plant divisions or rooted cuttings any time during the growing season.

BLUE STAR CREEPER

CREEPING RASPBERRY

PEACOCK MOSS

GOLDEN OREGANO

Botanical name: *Origanum vulgare* 'Aureum'

Range: Zones 5 to 9

Culture: Give this spreader lots of sun and good drainage. Plant divisions or rooted cuttings in the spring.

GOLDEN CREEPING THYME

Botanical name: *Thymus* × *citriodorus* 'Aureus'

Range: Zones 6 to 9

Culture: Native to the Mediterranean, it grows best in full sun and will endure only in well-drained soil. Amend average soil with sharp sand or course gravel to ensure good drainage. Plant divisions or rooted cuttings in the spring. Regular shearing improves air circulation and reduces fungal problems. Even when small sections of this ground cover die out, it bounces back quickly.

MAZUS REPTANS

Botanical name: *Mazus reptans*

Range: Zones 5 to 8

Culture: Plant it in shade for the best performance, but it also grows well in full sun as long as it's in moist soil. Plant divisions any time in the growing season or rooted cuttings in the spring.

PEACOCK MOSS

Botanical name: *Selaginella uncinata*

Range: Zones 7 to 11

Culture: Grow in moist woodland soil. Transplant pieces of stems where roots have formed any time in the growing season, or plant divisions in the spring. If the frondlike tips dry out or die back in winter, simply cut them back in early spring to expose the colorful new growth.

> *"For the impatient gardener, Mazus reptans fills in quickly, but is well-behaved."*
>
> ༄

yard, where it has managed to survive abuse from both two-legged and four-legged creatures. It's also a good alternative to creeping junipers along a steep slope. Quick to spread, its brown hairy stems put down roots wherever they touch the soil.

Evergreen in my Atlanta garden, creeping raspberry has rough, thick-textured leaves that are rounded with irregular edges. Up to 1½ in. in diameter, they start out rich green in spring. When cool fall weather arrives, some leaves take on tinges of orange, red, and then bronze, persisting through the winter. The underside of the leaves look as if they've been spray-painted bronze.

When I think of Australian plants, I conjure images of rugged, robust survivors. While blue star creeper (*Laurentia fluviatilis*), a native of Australia, is tough and easy to grow, it boasts a sweet and diminutive appearance that reminds me of baby's tears (*Soleirolia soleirolii*). On and off during spring and summer, delicate, sky-blue, star-shaped flowers appear amid tiny, bright-green leaves that are usually less than ¼ in. wide. Blue star creeper makes an attractive ground cover under trees and between stepping stones.

For the impatient gardener, *Mazus reptans* fills in quickly, but is well-behaved. It hugs the ground to form a tight carpet. In spring, tiny snapdragon-like blooms give the effect of a miniature flower garden. Blue or white with yellow markings, the blossoms rise up 2 in. to 4 in. above the foliage. Its many fibrous roots make it easy to propagate by division. Use this hardy perennial where its aggressive qualities

Golden creeping thyme spreads quickly around stepping stones. Its leaves release a lemony scent when brushed.

can be appreciated, such as between stepping stones or to cover large patches of soil. For an alluring combination, plant *Mazus reptans* along the edge of a pond with cardinal flower (*Lobelia cardinalis*).

OTHER GROUND COVERS SHOW OFF BEST IN THE SHADE

If you're looking for a rugged plant that will thrive even in boggy areas, try golden creeping Jenny (*Lysimachia nummularia* 'Aurea'). Also known as gold moneywort, this moisture lover puts out roots all along its stems so that large areas of ground are covered very quickly. Although the species is an aggressive grower in some areas, I've found that this cultivar is more well-behaved. Even so, you may want to curb its growth by creating barriers.

Golden creeping Jenny is also a good creeper to choke out weeds. Its shiny, rounded, yellow-green leaves light up an area and contrast well with dark-colored herbaceous plants like *Arum italicum* 'Pictum' and 'Palace Purple' alum root (*Heuchera micrantha* var. *diversifolia* 'Palace Purple').

More of a leaper than a creeper, 'Eco-Lacquered Spider' green-and-gold (*Chrysogonum virginianum* 'Eco-Lacquered Spider') is an outstanding new selection of this native species. It stands out with rosettes of blue-green, metallic-looking leaves, and small daisylike flowers about an inch in diameter. In winter, the foliage takes on tinges of purple. A fast grower, a one-gallon plant will cover an area five times as large in a single growing season. It sends out long, above-ground stolons that touch down and take root. For a stunning combination, plant 'Eco-Lacquered Spider' green-and-gold next to the charming, native dwarf crested iris (*Iris cristata*) which blooms around the same time.

Golden creeping Jenny's brilliant foliage looks stunning against dark-colored plants. This cultivar is more well-behaved than the species.

Another fine candidate for the woodland is peacock moss (*Selaginella uncinata*). With its tiny, fernlike, aquamarine-blue leaves, this plant looks almost prehistoric to me. Vigorous but not invasive, peacock moss forms tight mats of foliage that reach only 4 in. to 6 in. tall. This semi-evergreen perennial grows happily in combination with hellebores and ferns.

IT'S EASY TO GET GROUND COVERS GROWING

Ground-cover plantings are relatively easy to establish, whether you use seedlings, divisions, or rooted cuttings. Once you select an area to plant, prepare the soil in advance.

Since all the plants described in this chapter spread rather quickly, plant 2-in. to 3-in. seedlings or divisions on 6-in. centers. Apply a light layer of mulch to retain moisture and discourage weeds. Water new plantings daily until they become established, and then water according to the plant's moisture needs.

Planted Pockets
Give Life
to
Stone Walls

JENI WEBBER

is a residential landscape architect who has been designing gardens for 20 years. She studied horticulture at the University of Maryland and landscape architecture at the University of California, Berkeley.

Embellish existing walls with hens and chicks. Just stick a cutting in a crack and watch it take root. Plants with small root systems can also be used.

YOU HAVE TO APPROACH building stone walls a lot like you do life. When you hit stumbling blocks, look for creative opportunities. In wall building, those opportunities come when a rock fits well on all sides except one. Instead of launching a futile search for the perfect stone, just leave it alone. After all, the small gaps left from the not-quite-the-right-size rocks create perfect niches for rock-garden plants.

I learned to build walls from David Erdmann, a landscape contractor in Marin and Sonoma counties, California. He had, in turn, learned the craft as a teenager from an old stonemason working near Lake Tahoe. When David told me that I could put plants in the walls, I queried, "Really? Are you sure they will live?" Well, they did, and this has become my favorite form of wall building. I especially like the way plants settle the walls into the garden, giving them that characteristic, been-there-forever look.

"Rock crevices create a favorable environment for growing plants that would not normally survive in your zone."

∽

COVER IMPERFECTIONS IN WALLS WITH CASCADING PLANTS

Building a finely fitted stone wall is a craft that takes time and persistence to develop. In fact, many people choose not to tackle a stone wall as a garden project because it seems too daunting a task to lift the rocks, let alone to fit the rocks so tightly together. There are no

(RIGHT AND BELOW) Tuck cascading plants into crevices and let them spill over the top of retaining walls, which softens the appearance of the stone.

shortcuts to this craft, but there are ways to get around the obstacles.

First, select stones that suit your lifting ability. If you scale the size of the rocks down, building a wall is more like fitting together a jigsaw puzzle. And second, instead of fitting the stones together so tightly, adopt a method practiced in England at the turn of the century: fill gaps with small, crevice-loving plants. (For tips on building a dry-stacked stone retaining wall, see the sidebar on p. 76.)

Rock crevices create a favorable environment for growing plants that would not normally survive in your zone. The plants in these pockets are kept warmer and less waterlogged in the winter, and cooler and moister in the summer. The wall has an overall moderating effect on the climate, providing a perfect place for alpine plants, succulents, and herbs.

Although it's possible to grow plants in a freestanding wall, retaining walls are better suited for plantings because the earth behind a retaining wall supplies moisture to the planting pockets. They are also easier to build because the soil behind them provides good backing for the wall.

SECURE A SLOPE WITH STONES FOR A MODIFIED ROCK GARDEN

Rather than building a stacked stone wall, you can place a single layer of rock directly onto a slope to prevent erosion and create a modified rock garden. Start by digging a trench approximately 4 in. deep at the bottom of the grade, and secure your largest rocks in this trench. Then place a second course of rocks on top, angling them into the slope. Wiggle the stones back and forth to make sure they will not roll out, then repeat this process as you cover your hillside.

It's best to plant as you go, filling gaps with loose, loamy soil and an assortment of plants—

from larger, spreading plants to smaller, crevice-enhancing ones. Because this approach is not as precise as building a dry-stacked wall, you can use plants with larger root systems. Just be careful placing the next row of rocks so that you don't damage the roots of your plants.

SMALL, SPREADING PLANTS ARE MOST SUITABLE

Plants that do well in a rock wall are varied in nature—from small, delicately leaved, creeping plants like woolly creeping thyme (*Thymus pseudolanuginosus*) or prostrate rosemary (*Rosmarinus officinalis*); to drought-tolerant plants with minimal root systems like hens and chicks (*Echeveria* 'Imbricata') or other succulents; to tough, forgiving annuals such as wallflowers (*Erysimum cheiri*), trailing *Lobelia erinus*, and snapdragons (*Antirrhinum majus*) that reseed themselves from year to year. Your choice will be dictated by your hardiness zone and the aspect of your wall—whether it faces the sun or is sheltered in shade. You can often push the envelope when it comes to plant har-

Stone walls need not be drab. Brighten them with pockets of colorful flowering plants like this lobelia.

diness, as retaining walls tend to create a more moderate microclimate.

As they grow, creeping plants will cover much of the wall's surface, so don't overplant or you will lose the beauty of the stone. Also, be judicious with prolific spreaders and with plants that reseed themselves abundantly. Here in California, baby's tears (*Soleirolia soleirolii*) is the kudzu of the living wall. Once established, it flourishes in every damp

Retaining walls level a sloped site and provide plenty of places for planting. This wall is filled with fragrant herbs like rosemary and thyme.

Add stones to a slope for erosion control, creating planting pockets as you go. Fill the pocket with garden soil, add the plant (ABOVE), and then carefully secure the next stone (RIGHT).

crevice, obliterating a wall in a season or two if not controlled.

As a general rule, purchase young plants whose roots will easily fit in the planting pockets. And stick with plants that won't grow too large as they mature. Not only can large plants look out of proportion growing from a 3-ft. wall, but it will be more difficult for large plants to draw the water they need from the

"You can also add plants to existing walls, but they'll need to have tiny root systems."

soil in small planting pockets. I'd also suggest selecting drought-tolerant plants, as walls are usually quick-draining.

PACK PLANTING POCKETS WITH LOAMY GARDEN SOIL

To plant a pocket, wedge a small stone into the bottom front of the gap to create a miniature retaining wall that will keep soil from washing out. Next, take some well-amended soil and pack it into the pocket. This soil should be neither too clayey nor too gritty; a loamy soil is best. Ideally, the pocket will open out into the backfill, which will provide added moisture for plants and give their roots room for development. Spread the roots of your plant in the pocket, fill the rest of the hole with tightly packed soil, and water your planting.

You can also add plants to existing walls, but they'll need to have tiny root systems. Succulents with stems that poke into a hole and then take root are ideal. In time, they'll form a mat over the rocks. Use a stick or dibble to press soil into these holes, and wedge in a few pebbles to hold the soil in place.

IN DRY CLIMATES, WATER YOUR PLANTS FOR BEST RESULTS

One of the nice things about a stacked-stone wall or stone-secured slope is that, because of the angle, rainwater runs into cracks and crevices, reaching plant roots and soaking into the soil. In drier climates or during periods of drought, however, you'll have to water just as you would any garden.

Over the long haul, the easiest approach is to install an irrigation system. This can be done either as the wall is built or after it has been completed. One option is to run ½-gallon drip-irrigation emitters on ¼-in. tubing behind the wall and into the planting pockets while the wall is being built. The ¼-in. tubing is then

Plants for Walls

PERENNIALS FOR SUN

Aubrieta (*Aubrieta deltoidea*)

Baby's breath (*Gypsophila paniculata* 'Viette's Dwarf', *G. repens*)

Basket of gold (*Aurinia saxatilis*)

Bellflower (*Campanula isophylla*)

Blunt-lobed woodsia (*Woodsia obtusa*)

Candytuft (*Iberis sempervirens*)

Catnip (*Nepeta* × *faassenii*)

Columbine (*Aquilegia alpina*)

Hens and chicks (*Echeveria* 'Imbricata')

'Hidcote' lavender (*Lavandula angustifolia* 'Hidcote')

Moss pink (*Phlox subulata*)

Pinks (*Dianthus* cvs.)

Rock cress (*Arabis caucasica*)

Rosemary (*Rosmarinus officinalis* 'Prostratus')

Snow-in-summer (*Cerastium tomentosum*)

Stone cress (*Aethionema* 'Warley Rose')

Stone crop (*Sedum acre, S. spurium* 'Dragon's Blood')

Sun rose (*Helianthemum nummularium*)

Thyme (*Thymus herba-barona, T. praecox, T. pseudolanuginosus*)

PERENNIALS FOR SHADE

Baby's tears (*Soleirolia soleirolii*)

Bellflower (*Campanula poscharskyana, C. portenschlagiana*)

Columbine (*Aquilegia alpina*)

Creeping Jenny (*Lysimachia nummularia*)

House leek (*Sempervivum tectorum*)

Primrose (*Primula* × *polyantha, P. involucrata*)

Rupture-wort (*Herniaria glabra*)

Saxifrage (*Saxifraga umbrosa*)

ANNUALS FOR SUN OR SHADE

Snapdragon (*Antirrhinum majus*)

Sweet alyssum (*Lobularia maritima*)

Trailing lobelia (*Lobelia erinus*)

Wallflower (*Erysimum cheiri*)

connected to a ½-in. line near grade above the wall. Or simply run drip-emitter tubing with ½-gallon, in-line drip emitters at 1-ft. intervals at surface grade above the wall so that the water seeps into the backfill. Alternatively, spray irrigation (either low-volume, micro-spray heads or pop-up, full-pressure spray heads) can be used to wet the surface of the wall.

I water deeply up to twice a week in dry weather. By using drought-tolerant plants, you may be able to water less often. Get to know the needs of your plants and adjust your watering schedule accordingly. The result will be a lovely, long-lasting, planted wall.

Stone walls should slope back slightly for stability.

At 18 to 22 in., this wall doubles as garden seating.

Thyme loves the cool, well-drained conditions of a stone wall and fits nicely into planting pockets.

Stone walls drain quickly, so an irrigation system keeps plants watered during dry spells.

Build a Dry-Stacked Stone Retaining Wall

Once you have selected your site, you need to choose your stones. Look for rocks with angular faces—they stack better and a give a firmer repose. Rounded rocks are almost impossible to build into a wall without using copious amounts of mortar. An ideal rock has six parallel faces (like a brick). Regretfully, there aren't many ideal rocks available, so look for angular rocks with the most flat faces. To figure out how much stone you'll need, multiply your wall's height times the depth times the length. If your wall is 2 ft. high, 1 1/2 ft. wide, and 20 ft. long, you'll need roughly 60 cubic ft. of stone. Most stoneyards will deliver the stones for a slight charge. Be sure to have them placed as close to the site of your retaining wall as possible.

As for tools, you'll need a shovel for digging your trench and backfilling, a mattock for attacking the grade, and a small sledgehammer for tamping soil. For marking your site and leveling rocks, you'll need a line level, a few tall stakes, string, some flour, and a 4-ft. or 8-ft. level.

So you're all set with your tools, some drinking water, and maybe some tunes to work by. The first thing to do is to determine the front face of the wall. If it is straight, a board or a string stretched between stakes can be used to mark the line. Otherwise, use a garden hose and mark the edge with flour.

Now you can start digging. The easiest approach is to cut and fill—that is, dig into the slope where the wall will go and spread the earth below you to create a level terrace. When you cut and fill, the wall is backed by undisturbed soil, which is more stable than fill. For design reasons, however, you might choose to build a freestanding wall and fill behind it with soil from another site. Or you might do a partial cut and fill, which is somewhere between the two.

Walls are built in courses. The base course is structurally the most important, while the final course, the capstone, is the most challenging. For stability, walls should be at least 20 in. wide at the base. They can taper slightly toward the top, but you'll want a wall that is at least two rocks wide in most places. This can be accomplished by mixing stones of different sizes or by backfilling with a combination of two-thirds rubble to one-third soil.

DIG A TRENCH FOR THE BASE COURSE

Start by digging a trench about 4 in. deep and at least 2 ft. wide. A straight-edged spade will give you a nice, even edge. The first course must be very solid and tightly fit because the weight of the wall will rest on it. Take the time to find rocks that lock into place, without leaving gaps. Randomly lay your largest rocks along the front edge of the trench. Set the first stone, shifting it around until it sits securely without being rocked easily, and then fill with the remaining stones. If you are using rectangular stones, you want the height of adjacent stones to be the same, or of a difference that can be made up with a smaller stone. If the rocks are irregular, then the stones will fit together leaving a triangular gap for the next course to fit into. I find irregular rocks easier to work with than flat ones; with flat rocks you have to be more precise. Find a stone that fits well and then continue for a few more feet. A rule of thumb, passed down from my wall-building teacher's mentor, is to try a stone seven different ways. If it doesn't fit by the seventh try, use another stone.

Next, shovel dirt behind the stones and tamp the earth into the spaces between, behind, and beneath the stones with top of the sledgehammer. This is an important step because the dirt becomes the mortar for the wall. I also recommend adding rubble (those stones you won't use on the face of your wall) behind the face course to give greater strength to the wall. Pound the rubble and soil mix until you are satisfied that it is solid. Continue the first course until you reach the end of the wall. When you are done, test your course by walking gently on it. The stones should not roll out beneath your weight.

To begin the second course, choose a stone that will bridge the first joint of the bottom course. Avoid having joints run up the face of the wall, and angle (batter) the courses backward—approximately 1 in. per vertical foot. This creates a stable wall. For added strength, intermittently place single stones that run the full depth of the wall. This will only work with rectangular rocks. For irregular rocks, place a large rock behind a face rock every 3 ft. or so. As you set a course, you will come to situations, probably quite a few of them, where the rock placement is perfect on all sides but one. These are the planting opportunities that give life to a stone wall.

Continue building in this manner until you are one course away from the finished height. Fitting stones will get easier as you go, and you'll likely discover that there's a certain magic moment when you're building a wall: you hear a thump that signals you've placed a rock perfectly.

MAKE YOUR WALL SITTING HEIGHT

The ideal height for a dry-stacked retaining wall is 18 in. to 22 in.—so you can sit on it when your gardening chores are done. Even if you don't plan to sit on your wall, 3 ft. is about as high as I would recommend building any dry-stacked wall; higher walls should be engineered for stability.

Using your stakes, string, and line level, mark the height of the capstone. You'll also want to check the level of individual stones as you go. It's difficult to get the capstone perfectly level, but a 1-in. variance looks level overall.

Bring plenty of patience to the process of laying the capstone; it is a culmination of the skill you have developed to this point. It should be about 15 in. to 18 in. deep, made up of one to three stones. Use soil and good placement to secure the stones, and just as with wall joints, avoid lengthy joints in the capstone. If you want to sit on the wall, choose smooth, flat stones. Or, fill gaps with soil and plant fragrant herbs for cushions. A planted capstone is a delightful finishing touch to a living wall.

Section of Planted Wall

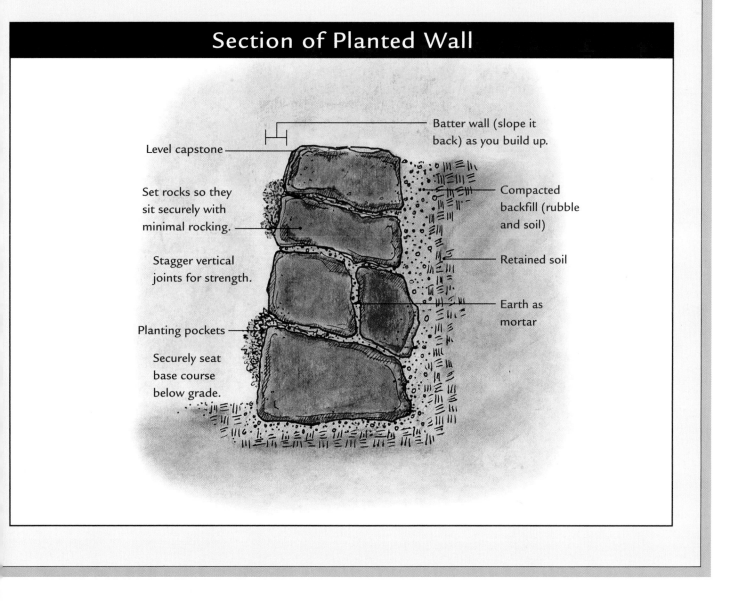

Batter wall (slope it back) as you build up.

Level capstone

Set rocks so they sit securely with minimal rocking.

Stagger vertical joints for strength.

Planting pockets

Securely seat base course below grade.

Compacted backfill (rubble and soil)

Retained soil

Earth as mortar

BARBARA BLOSSOM ASHMUN

is a garden designer, writer, and consultant. She is the author of several books, including *Garden Retreats* and *The Garden Design Primer*, and is a contributing editor for *Fine Gardening*.

Anchor Your Garden with Striking Annuals

(FAR LEFT) Perk up beds in transition. The substantial flowers of *Dahlia* 'Park Princess' function as able fillers between immature shrubs and perennials.

(NEAR LEFT) Uncommon specimens impress as focal points. The striking, coppery swords of New Zealand flax merit a front-row seat in the border.

THE FIRST TIME that I laid eyes on the bold leaves of castor bean (*Ricinus communis*) combined with white spider flowers (*Cleome hassleriana* 'Helen Campbell'), I stopped dead in my tracks. I was touring gardens in Canada, but this vignette looked like a Tahitian jungle scene from a Gauguin painting. The annual castor bean plants were tall and sumptuous, with what looked like very large, chocolate-colored maple leaves. The annual spider flowers also had tropical-looking foliage, but it was their long, thin stamens, sticking out like cat whiskers, that caught my fancy.

Unlike annuals such as petunias and zinnias, which are mainly grown for color, castor beans and spider flowers have foliage, flowers, and architectural structure that make strong statements in the garden. Best of all, they provide all this drama in just one growing season. When dealing with new beds and designs, they provide a quick fix of colorful structure.

It's important when choosing an architectural annual to consider its growth habit. To help evaluate whether a plant grows narrowly upright or spreads, squint to see its silhouette. Then, fit the plant to a place that will benefit from its shape. Use upright forms as backdrops for other plants, and spreaders as quick border fillers.

Upright architectural annuals like castor beans—with big, dramatic leaves and eye-catching, late-summer, red flower spikes—make excellent backdrops for flowers that are short on foliage such as asters (*Aster × frikartii*) and red-hot pokers (*Kniphofia* cvs.). Also, the castor bean's upright shape is a perfect foil for the more billowy masses of tickseed (*Coreopsis verticillata* 'Moonbeam') that can look a little lost without a companion to anchor them. The red-leaved castor bean cultivars 'Carmencita' and 'Sanguineus' are especially striking with *Lobelia cardinalis* and *Achillea* 'Salmon Beauty'. The castor bean's only drawback is that the spotted seeds it produces in late summer are poisonous if eaten, so remove the flowers before they form seedpods.

Love-lies-bleeding (*Amaranthus caudatus*) spreads to 5 ft., filling an area nearly as wide as it rises. The showy, red tassels that cascade from the tips of its branches make it a great focal point also. It's a specimen plant that that deserves a special place in the garden where its assertiveness and stature will be appreciated. Plant *Sedum spurium* 'Dragon's Blood'—with its dark-red leaves and bright, pinkish-red

(LEFT) Unusual annuals are attention-getters. The gigantic size and unusual shape of the castor bean's leaves make it a focal point in the garden.

(OPPOSITE) Indulge your urge to experiment. The showy, red tassels of love-lies-bleeding create a dazzling display.

> *"To help evaluate whether a plant grows narrowly upright or spreads, squint to see its silhouette."*

flowers—or *Sedum* 'Vera Jameson'—with its dusky leaves and dusty pink flowers—for a plush carpet of thick, fleshy leaves at its feet.

FANCY, FLAMBOYANT ANNUALS PERFORM WELL AS FILLERS

When young beds with newly planted shrubs and perennials look sparse, fill in the gaps with annuals until the permanent plants grow up. For instance, voluptuous, summer-blooming dahlias (*Dahlia* spp.) pacified me during the three years it took for my roses to fully mature. Although technically a perennial to USDA Hardiness Zone 8, dahlias—especially pompom dahlias—are great to use as temporary fillers between shrubs or perennials. I'm particularly fond of maroon 'Crossfield Ebony' as a dark accent.

Annual flowering tobaccos (*Nicotiana alata* cvs.) are spreaders that make fine fillers. Their delicate, funnel-shaped flowers blend well with neighbors and give a good drift of color. Pink, red, and white flowers are most common, but I favor the subtle 'Lime Green', which is the best blender. For a more exotic-looking, upright, flowering tobacco, *N. sylvestris*—with its oversize leaves and pendant clusters of white, scented flowers—is guaranteed to be a conversation piece.

Some annuals are wonderful weavers that knit disparate parts of the composition together and link neighboring plants into a coherent community. White laceflowers (*Ammi*

Anchor designs with upright plants. *Nicotiana sylvestris* makes a perfect backdrop for *Verbena* 'Linda'.

majus)—which look like a more refined version of Queen Anne's lace—are just what's needed to unite a bed of shrub roses. Masses of lavender *Verbena bonariensis*, whose form mimics a candelabra with its sturdy main stem and angled branches, blend well with hot-pink hybrid roses such as *Rosa* 'Vanity'. Although *V. bonariensis* is hardy to Zone 7 as a perennial, it makes a dazzling annual in colder areas.

TALL ANNUALS FORM QUICK AND COLORFUL HEDGES

For quick, colorful hedges to increase privacy, use upright annuals such as spider flowers, sunflowers (*Helianthus annuus*), and cosmos (*Cosmos bipinnatus*). Mix spider flowers and cosmos to make a tall, blooming wall in shades of pink, white, and violet. If you prefer warmer colors, the vibrant orange blooms of torch flowers (*Tithonia rotundifolia*) strike a wallop when combined with hedge-high 'Moonwalker', 'Velvet Queen', 'Prado Red', or 'Sunburst Mixed' sunflower varieties.

Although it will bloom only in tropical areas, the leaves alone are worth the trouble of seeking out *Hibiscus acetosella* 'Red Shield'. Technically a perennial to Zone 10, its elegantly cut foliage reminds me of red-leaved Japanese maples. Picture a hedge of this as the backdrop for a bed of chartreuse-flowering *Nicotiana langsdorfii* and green bells of Ireland (*Moluccella laevis*).

USE INTRIGUING SPECIMENS AS FOCAL POINTS

Angel's trumpet (*Brugmansia* spp.) is an annual that is best used as an architectural specimen plant. Its white, lavender, or peach flowers are knockouts that make great focal points in a border. Leaves as large as a magnolia's and an enticing evening scent also add interest.

> *"Mix spider flowers and cosmos to make a tall, blooming wall in shades of pink, white, and violet."*

New Zealand flax (*Phormium tenax*), which is considered to be a perennial to Zone 8, shows off its best qualities as an architectural specimen. Its geometric shape and intriguingly colored foliage—whether chocolate-brown or striped cream, pink, and green—make this plant a standout. Quiet, small-textured underpinnings such as blue Swan River daisy (*Brachycome iberidifolia*) or 'Silver Brocade' artemisia (*A. stelleriana* 'Silver Brocade') are suitably subtle sidekicks.

UNUSUAL ANNUALS MAKE BOLD STATEMENTS IN CONTAINERS

Growing unusual annuals in containers draws more attention to them. This is especially helpful when the flowers are subtle colors that can be easily lost in a border, or very dark colors that tend to disappear in the midst of other flowers. A single specimen of the pale green-flowering love-lies-bleeding (*A. caudatus* 'Viridis') in a terra-cotta pot makes a much stronger statement on its own than one jumbled up in a border. A red-leaved castor bean in a gray container paints a vivid picture when solo, even though the plant won't reach the height that it would in the ground.

Annuals encourage me to experiment. After all, they're here for only a short time, so I don't need to take them as seriously as other long-term investments like trees and shrubs. I love the quick thrill of watching them explode in one growing season. As long as I have new beds and borders to develop, architectural annuals will be my instant bones.

JUDITH R. GRIES

is a garden design consultant. She owns a small nursery that features carefree and hardy roses and companion perennials, and she also lectures about gardening with her husband, Robert Gries.

Creating
an
Allée
through Your Garden

Traditionally, allées, or tree-lined avenues, were reserved for the grandest of estates. But Judith Gries proves they are just as inviting in small gardens.

ONCE UPON A TIME, I was Alice in Wonderland, Peter Pan, Pocahontas—even a member of the Swiss Family Robinson, living high in a tree house. Back then, in my younger days, I had what you might call an active imagination. In pursuit of my childhood fantasies, I created trails, designed huts, and climbed into soaring trees. These hideaways became my secret places, private paradises where I could wish upon a star or revel in the wonder of nature.

When I grew up, my love for creating and designing led me to gardening. And when I discovered the garden styles of England, I liked them immediately. English gardens seem to echo the places I loved as a child—they are intimate and full of mystery, with vistas and surprises around each bend. Their pathways—arranged to conceal, then reveal, a statue, a vista, or a simple garden bench—lure you from one scene to the next. And the best of the pathways were

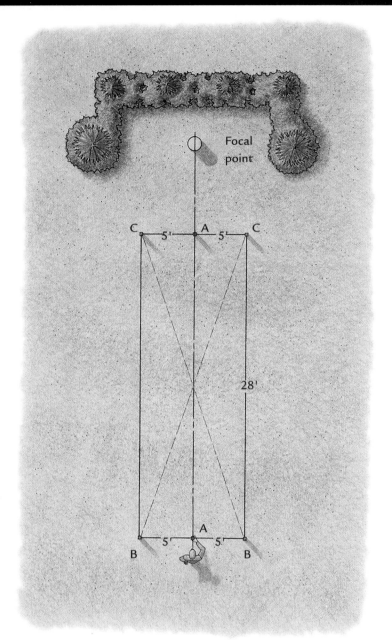

Focal point

C 5' A 5' C

28'

A

B 5' 5' B

Set up stakes (A) at the front and back of the allée's desired course, and sight along them to make sure they direct the eye to a desired focal point. Then, using stakes and string, mark the corners of the allée (B and C) and the lines where the trees would be planted (B to C). The tree-planting lines should be parallel with, and equidistant to, the sight line. Measure the diagonal lines; if they are of equal length, the allée is symmetrical. Finally, check the allée's course by eye to make sure it is pleasing. Then, if anything looks out of place, move it.

the allées, those long, tree-lined walkways that parade through the gardens with crisp, well-mannered formality.

The allées I admired were always on a grand scale, with wide promenades and twin ranks of towering trees spaced as precisely as pickets in a fence. They usually graced only the grandest of estates. Our country, Federal-style house in northeast Connecticut was rather humble by comparison, but I so loved allées that I was determined to add one to my acre of yew- and beech-hedged garden rooms. I just didn't know if they would work in my miniature landscape.

I've since learned that they do. In fact, I think they work so well in a small garden that I just planted a third allée in my yard. It's only 10 ft. wide and not even 30 ft. long, but it seems much bigger. The secret, I've found, is using small trees and forcing the perspective—planting in rows that are not quite parallel and staggering the spacing between the trees in each row so that those in the background are closer together than those in the front of the allée. The combined effect makes even a pint-size allée look like a long, leafy hallway leading off into the distance.

Allées bring a special touch to any garden. Their rigorously formal lines impose pattern upon the garden, and their height creates an often needed vertical accent. There's something compelling about walking through an allée—the rhythmic repetition of trees beckons you onward.

CHOOSE TREES THAT MARK THE PASSING OF SEASONS

Allées can be made with shrubs, evergreens, or even columns of wood or stone, but I like to use deciduous trees because they seem to celebrate the passing of the seasons. In spring, there are bright blossoms; in summer, lush greenery; and in fall, the changing colors of the foliage. In winter, the bare skeletons of the trees become snow-laden silhouettes etched against the winter sky.

Each of our three allées looks distinctive, thanks, in large part, to the different trees we've used. The trees in our allée of ornamental pears will soon grow together to form a single overhead canopy, like a leafy, green archway. Our allée of pyramidal European hornbeam (*Carpinus betulus* 'Fastigiata') will be groomed and pruned to look almost like topiary—I plan to pleach the trees to make a sort of hedge on stilts. Our newest allée is planted with 'Red Baron' crabapples (*Malus* 'Red Baron') that will grow 12 ft. to 15 ft. tall, with a spread of 6 ft. In time they will form an allée composed of individual specimens rather than a mass of trees grown into one another. Using our newest allée as an example, I'll explain how my husband, Robert, and I plan and plant these formal avenues in small gardens.

GIVE YOUR ALLÉE A DESTINATION

Whatever trees are used, I think allées are most effective as passageways connecting one garden room to another. They can also be used to frame a scenic vista, a statue, or any garden focal point. Allées should lead somewhere and, in planning, it helps to think of them as a one-way path. That way you can take real advantage of a forced perspective and use it to draw viewers toward whatever focal point you want to highlight. However you use them, allées are destined to be rather permanent garden features; since you're not likely to transplant the trees in an allée, it's especially important to site them with care.

Once I have an idea about where to place an allée, I place a stake at either end of the proposed planting, right in the middle of what will be the pathway through the allée. Then, I make sure that sighting along the two stakes

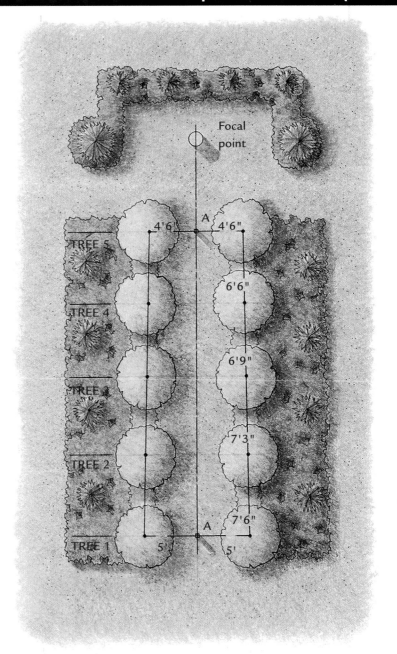

Leaving the entry to the allée at full width, reduce the distance between the two trees at the back and move the rear stakes, which will mark the new positions for tree 5. Measure the diagonals to check for symmetry. Realign the strings marking the two rows where the trees will be planted to reflect the new, slightly tapered pattern. Set stakes for tree 2, tree 3, and tree 4 as marked, so the distance between each one decreases toward the back of the allée. Measure diagonals between trees 1 and 2, 2 and 3, 3 and 4, and 4 and 5 to ensure symmetry.

directs my eye to the intended destination. If they don't, we move the stakes until they do.

USE MATH TO PLAN THE BASIC DESIGN

When we know where to put the allée, Robert, a mathematician, uses simple arithmetic to plot out a planting area. It's not solely an exercise in number-crunching. As Robert likes to say, allées are done partly in the head and partly in the heart. We use our heads to make precise mathematic measurements and set a stake to represent the place where each tree will stand. Then we use our hearts to rearrange the stakes if the arithmetic allée doesn't feel quite right.

We determine the width and length for an allée by using the mature spread of its trees as a guide for spacing both the rows and the trees lining each row. We are also careful to factor in the look we want for the allée. Our crabapples will grow to 6 ft. across, and since we want them to remain as individual specimens, we will have to plant the rows more than 6 ft. apart. For a different look, we could plant the rows less than 6 ft. apart and let the trees grow into one another to form a single canopy over the allée. Rows planted that closely together don't leave much space for path, so I think wider-canopied trees, such as ornamental pears, are best for making tunnel-like allées.

Allées provide a dramatic frame for a garden focal point. The formal lines of this ornamental pear allée direct a viewer's gaze.

> *"I think wider-canopied trees, such as ornamental pears, are best for making tunnel-like allées."*

We have another, more personal consideration for planning the width of our crabapple allée: We want to be able drive a vehicle through it. So, we decide to space the rows a generous 10 ft. apart. Even if we didn't need that much space, we would still add a few extra feet to the tree's 6-ft. width so that the allée wouldn't seem too claustrophobic. It depends on the trees and the design, but the rows in any allée should be at least 8 ft. apart.

To determine the allée's length, we begin again with the crabapple's mature spread, 6 ft. We know we want to plant the trees a little farther apart than that, so they remain distinct even when full grown. We decide to space them 7 ft. apart, leaving just a little space between each mature tree.

With the spacing between the trees in each row decided, calculating the length of each row is simple as long as you know one of two things: how many trees you want in each row, or how long an area you want to fill. Space was tight for our crabapple allée, but we wanted at least five trees in each row. To me, that's the minimum. An allée with four trees to a row might look pleasing, but, like classical designers since the time of the ancient Greeks, we prefer to use odd numbers in our designs. To figure the length of the allée, we multiply the feet of spacing between trees (7), times the number of trees we want, less one (4). We subtract one from the actual number of trees because half of the tree at each end will be outside the planting area we are calculating. Anyway, 4 multiplied by 7 is 28. So, according

to the math, our allée will consist of two 28-ft. rows of five trees planted 7 ft. apart.

Or, if we know the length we want but aren't sure how many trees to plant, we divide the overall length by the distance between each tree, then add one—we need to put back the two halves we removed in the earlier calculation—for a final count. For example, a 70-ft.-long area with trees 7 ft. apart, would need 10 plus 1, or 11, trees per row.

STAKE OUT THE PLANTING AREA

With our allée's 28-ft. length and 10-ft. width decided, we return to the two stakes set up for siting the allée and rearrange them so they are 28 ft. apart. Again, we check to make sure the sight line is what we want. If it's not, we move the stakes, as long as they remain 28 ft. apart.

Those two stakes mark what will be the middle of our pathway once the allée is planted. In order to create a good home for the trees, as well as for the shrubs and perennials we will eventually plant under them, we till and amend a generous swath of soil on either side of the center line, leaving a few untouched feet in the middle for the walkway. There's no need to be too precise here—edging and planting grass seed can be done after the allée is in place. Then, using another pair of stakes, we mark the planting spot for the first tree in each row of the allée. These will be located 5 ft. to the right and left, respectively, of the stake we set up earlier to site the allée. Then we set two more stakes at the back of each row; each one of them should be 28 ft. from the front stake in the same row. To make

Low-Growing Hedge Plants Complete the Effect

To heighten the hallway effect of an allée and to provide a feeling of depth and variety, I plant hedges of shade-tolerant shrubs just outside the two rows of trees.

Some of my favorite hedging shrubs include Mento barberry *(Berberis × mentorensis)*, a superior hedge plant with tiny, golden-yellow, spring flowers; dwarf, winged euonymous *(Euonymus alatus* 'Compactus'), with its fiery-red fall foliage; and *Ribes alpinum*, an ornamental currant densely covered with tiny, glossy leaves.

I also like to use perennials to help give the planting substance. While the trees are still whips, I plant daylilies along the outer borders of the allée to help define the area. But as the trees grow and create more shade, I move the daylilies to another part of the garden and replace them with large-leaved, shade-tolerant hostas. Directly under the allée, I like to use lady's mantle, with its late spring clusters of yellow flowers, and sweet woodruff, which bears white flowers in May. I also like to use goatsbeard, lily of the valley, bleeding heart, and 'Palace Purple' coralbells *(Heuchera americana* 'Palace Purple') paired with creeping Jenny *(Lysimachia nummularia* 'Aurea').

Even once it's all planted, you can't hurry an allée. It will be a good three years before the whips grow enough to start looking like an allée. But I'm patient—I know the trees will gradually mature, and the allée will become one of my garden's most striking features.

---

sure the rectangle formed by the four outer stakes is symmetrical, we use the old carpenter's trick of measuring the diagonals. Each one should be the same length.

With the four corner stakes positioned properly, we stretch a length of string from the front stake to the back stake on each side. Then we walk back and forth through our proposed allée, viewing it from all vantage points. If there's something we don't like, or if the allée seems like it should be moved this way or that, we make adjustments.

MAKE A SMALL ALLÉE LOOK LONGER BY FORCING THE PERSPECTIVE

So far, so good. Now it gets a little tricky. An allée 28 ft. long isn't going to look very substantial unless we force the perspective to make it appear to be longer. Forcing the perspective may sound complicated, but it's not. If you've ever drawn a picture of a road receding into the distance until it disappears at a single point, you've already forced perspective. Be careful when employing this technique—it's easy to go too far and make the allée look out-of-kilter.

Perspective can be forced in only one direction, so it's easiest to begin at the front entry to the allée and work toward the focal point it leads to. The idea is to make the rows converge slightly toward the back of the allée and to space the trees so that they get progressively closer together the farther back you go in each row. For simplicity's sake, it helps to identify the trees in our two rows of five trees. We'll call the trees at the entrance tree 1, and the trees at the back tree 5. Counting from front to back, we have trees 1, 2, 3, 4, and 5.

We've found that even the smallest changes in the distance between rows can have a big effect. The idea is to force the perspective just enough to get the illusion, but not so much that the planting appears misaligned. For our

"The idea is to make the rows converge slightly toward the back of the allée."

28-ft. allée, we decided to make the two trees at the back (tree 5) a foot closer together than the two trees at the front (tree 1). We would not want them any closer together for an allée this short. Otherwise, if you looked from the back to the front of the allée, the effect would be ruined because the two rows of trees would no longer appear to be parallel. We reposition the two stakes at the back to get a sense of how it will look, and adjust them if necessary. When they are in place, we check the symmetry again by measuring the diagonals. When they match, we stretch a length of twine along each of the two long sides of our former rectangle, which is now, in geometric terms, a trapezoid. Every tree in the allée will be planted along those two lines.

To get the full effect of a forced perspective, we also vary the distance between the trees in each row. Instead of planting one tree in the corner, and one every 7 ft. until the fifth tree is planted 28 ft. from the first, we plant foreground trees farther apart than those toward the back.

Again, subtle differences yield big results. So instead of planting trees 2 and 4 exactly 7 ft. in from each of the corner stakes, we put the tree 2 an extra 6 in. farther away, at 7½ ft. from tree 1. We compensate for that extra 6 in. by planting tree 4 only 6½ ft. from tree 5. That leaves us with 14 ft. between trees 2 and 4. But as you probably guessed, we don't plant the center tree (tree 3) in the middle. To determine its location, we halve the 6-in. difference we used earlier, and plant tree 3 a few inches off-center, 14 ft. and 9 in. from the tree in front (tree 1) and 13 ft. and 3 in. from the tree in back (tree 5).

Mark the locations with stakes, and again check the symmetry by measuring all the diagonals. Now, walk back and forth through the allée. Try to get a feel for what it will look like

with trees. If something looks out of place, move it until it looks right. Despite the precise calculations, the most important thing is that the allée *looks* right. Once it does, we put away the pencil and paper, and get out the shovel.

PLANT WHIPS AND TRIM OFF THEIR BRANCHES

We plant whips—young, almost branchless saplings—because they are inexpensive, grow quickly, and are easy to train. The twine stretched along each row serves as our guide for planting the whips. We also carefully remove the stakes that mark each tree and lay them down so that they point to the planting spot they formerly marked. That way, we don't need to do any more measuring.

To encourage the young trees, we dig a generously sized, deep planting hole, add bonemeal or superphosphate for root growth, and plant the whips so the grafts are below ground level. Then we trim them to 5 ft. tall and remove any side shoots or branches. If the whips are less than 5 ft. tall, we just remove the side shoots. Finally, we tie and stake them. As the season progresses, and in future years, we continue to pinch off any new branches below the 4-ft. or 5-ft. level to allow room for people to walk. Soon enough the trees will grow, their canopies will spread, and once again I'll be able to set off on hidden pathways.

Enhance an allée by underplanting it with shade-tolerant shrubs and perennials. Using ground covers, edging plants, and shrub hedges gives an allée a feeling of greater depth and substance.

ISIS SPINOLA-SCHWARTZ

is principal of Schwartz and Associates, a landscape architecture firm in Mill Valley, California, specializing in planning and analysis, and residential landscape design. She is a member of the American Society of Landscape Architects.

Planted Paths

Define Garden Spaces

Paths can separate gardens from lawns. Planting between the flagstones helps create a soft transition.

IT'S OFTEN BEEN SAID that the journey is more important than the destination. My husband, David, and I have been using that principle in our landscape-architecture practice for years now. Many people think of paths primarily as a means of getting from one point to another. Although we use paths for that purpose, we also use them as transitional elements between different parts of a garden—whether a patio and a lawn, a perennial border and a meadow, or, most recently, between a formal garden and an apple orchard. A path used in this way—as an edge or border—encourages people to stop along the way and take in the beauty all around.

A neat, crisp path would be too harsh a transition, though, so in between the stone, wood, or concrete pavers, we use plants to soften the path visually. These plantings often obscure the edges of the path, resulting in a looser, more naturalistic look. Sometimes we use a plant in the

Lush, but not thirsty.
The succulents along
these redwood rounds
are well-suited to arid
climates and show
another way of
approaching a planted
path.

path that we've also used in an adjacent bed or border. This tends to blur the line between the path and the planting, making the path—though a distinctly separate garden element—almost an extension of the planting.

Our use of paths as transitional elements actually began on a more utilitarian note. Gardens do tend to be more laid-back here on the West Coast than in the east, but laid-back doesn't mean sloppy. We like to be able to get around our gardens, even in winter when the ground is soggy, to take care of weeding, pruning, and other maintenance. David and I started putting in these paths along the tops and bottoms of planted slopes, so we could get to the plantings without sloshing through mud or wet grass. Our use of these paths gradually increased as we realized how useful and handsome they were throughout the garden. Today these paths feature prominently in most of the gardens we design. Over the years, many of our clients have told us that they appreciate being able to walk through their gardens, regardless of the season, without changing from street shoes into gardening boots.

CHOOSE INFORMAL PAVERS LIKE FLAGSTONES

Because the overall look of these paths is informal, we've always used pavers that underscored that same image. Various kinds of flagstone, with their irregular edges, work well. In milder climates, redwood or cedar rounds—transverse sections from a tree—look quite at home. Surprisingly, precast concrete pavers also work well, quickly gaining a patina and becoming partially obscured by a ground cover between the individual pavers as well as by larger, mounding plants, which tend to spill over onto them.

"Our use of these paths gradually increased as we realized how useful and handsome they were throughout the garden."

We always use larger pavers (12 in. square would be about the smallest) because they provide a firm, sure step. To provide planting pockets, we generally leave at least 3 in. to 4 in. between pavers.

In a large garden, we often use several different paving materials. However, we use only one material in each area. This helps both to differentiate parts of a garden from one another and to create a sense of unity within each section.

Sometimes these edging paths are straight, but more often they curve or wind around planting beds or other garden features. Because the paving materials used are informal and the spacing between pavers is wide, it's no more difficult putting in a curved path than a straight one.

Regardless of path configuration, it's necessary to put a foundation of sorts beneath the pavers, so they don't settle or shift. We use a number of different bases beneath the pavers depending on the site and the client's tastes, but the base we use most often, a two-layer affair of crushed stone and compacted sand that ensures good drainage and excellent support for the pavers, will work well in almost any situation.

Simple Steps to Planted Paths

A planted stepping stone path doesn't have to be a difficult or intimidating project. Sure, there's work involved—digging, tamping, and some hauling—but the process itself isn't overly complex. The two most important factors for a long-lasting path are adequate drainage and solid, even support for the pavers.

1 Remove any existing grass or surface material to a depth of about 5 in. below the desired finished level.

2 Firmly tamp the soil to create a solid base.

3 Lay 3 in. of mixed gravel and crushed stone (often called rock fines) to provide good drainage. Tamp into place.

4 Spread 1 in. of coarse builder's sand over the gravel and crushed stone. Smooth it out and tamp.

5 Set the pavers in place, leaving 3 in. to 4 in. between each one. Press and twist each into a snug, level position.

6 Fill the cracks between the pavers and the area around them with a roughly 50-50 mix of sand and topsoil.

7 Spread grass seed and plant your low-growing or creeping plants in this sand and soil mix. Water well until plants are established. Finish with a layer of mulch.

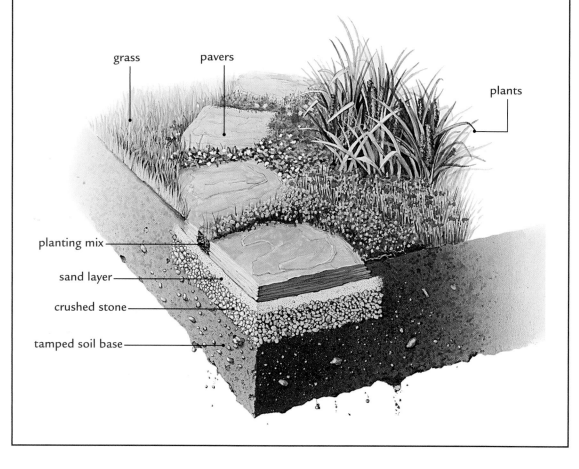

grass   pavers   plants

planting mix
sand layer
crushed stone
tamped soil base

CHEERFUL, LOW-GROWING PLANTS AND CREEPERS COMPLETE THE COMPOSITION

The plants we use in our pathways fall into two categories, roughly speaking—those we plant right in the paths and those that we generally place at or near the edges of the paths. All of these plants work both to soften the look of the pavers and to give the paths a more established, mature appearance.

When choosing plants for use in the paths I look for those that are soft to walk on, have some visual interest (flowers or foliage texture), and are easily maintained. For instance, I like chamomile (*Chamaemelum nobile*) because of its fine texture and the feeling that

(ABOVE AND LEFT) Steps are paths with altitude, and they provide dramatic opportunities for planting. The plants not only soften the stone visually but also give the steps an established, been-here-forever look.

Mix plants of different sizes along your pathway. Tiny creepers like thyme and Corsican mint can fill the cracks, while medium-sized perennials like this sedum spill in from the side.

I am walking on a soft carpet as I step on it. The little yellow flowers are attractive, too, both to people and insects. Wild strawberry and sedums are used for their sturdiness. Another favorite is pink-flowered knotweed (*Polygonum capitatum*), for its bronze leaves, small pink flowers, and the ease with which it's propagated. Carpet bugle weed (*Ajuga reptans*) and blue-star creeper (*Laurentia fluviatilis*) are my favorite shade plants—both have great texture, color, and the ability to withstand a lot of foot traffic.

Along the edges of the paths, there are many plants we use on a regular basis, but

I will add plants to the palette any time I discover something new and wonderful. I often select plants for the edges that complement the garden, patio, or whatever else is adjacent to the path.

For informal edges, we often use Penstemon gloxinioides, maiden pink (*Dianthus deltoides*), fleabane (*Erigeron compositus*), cranesbill (*Geranium sanguineum* and G. 'Johnson's Blue'), rock rose (*Cistus* × *purpureus* and *C. hybridus*), silvermound (*Artemisia schmidtiana*), spurge (*Euphorbia* × *martinii*), and lamb's ears (*Stachys byzantina*). For slightly more formal edges, we commonly use *Lantana montevidensis* and *L. camara*, fringed lavender (*Lavandula dentata*), lilyturf (*Liriope muscari*), and *Astilbe chinensis* var. *pumila*.

Occasionally, we also use very striking plants at the beginning of a path, at the base of steps, and in other transitional areas of the garden. Plants like New Zealand flax (*Phormium tenax*), *Dietes iridioides* and *D. bicolor*, giant feather grass (*Stipa gigantea*), and kangaroo paw (*Anigozanthos flavidus*) all make dramatic accents.

The thing to remember in creating a planted garden path is, above all, to keep yourself open to the possibilities. We're constantly trying new plants or combinations, both for ourselves and for our clients. Choosing plants is the most enjoyable part of putting in a planted path.

"I like chamomile because of its fine texture and the feeling that I am walking on a soft carpet as I step on it."

Plants for Paths

IN PATH, SHADY

Ajuga reptans (carpet bugle weed)

Fragaria chiloensis (beach strawberry)

Lamium maculatum 'White Nancy'
   (spotted dead nettle)

Laurentia fluviatilis (blue-star creeper)

Ophiopogon japonicus (mondo grass)

Oxalis oregana (redwood sorrel)

Phlox subulata (creeping phlox)

Sagina subulata 'Aurea' (golden pearlwort)

IN PATH, SUN TO PARTIAL SHADE

Armeria maritima (sea thrift)

Carex flacca (blue sedge)

Cerastium tomentosum (snow-in-summer)

Chamaemelum nobile (chamomile)

Festuca ovina 'Glauca Minima' (sheep fescue)

Origanum vulgare 'Aureum' (creeping oregano)

Sedum acre (golden moss or golden carpet)

Thymus spp. (creeping thyme)

PATH EDGE, SHADY

Alchemilla spp. (lady's mantle)

Astilbe chinensis (astilbe)

Bergenia cordifolia (bergenia)

Dianthus deltoides (maiden pink)

Galium odoratum (sweet woodruff)

Helleborus spp. (hellebore)

Hemerocallis spp. (daylily)

Liriope muscari (lilyturf)

Penstemon gloxinioides (penstemon)

Polystichum munitum (Western sword fern)

PATH EDGE, SUN TO PARTIAL SHADE

Artemisia schmidtiana (silver mound)

Ceanothus 'Julia Phelps' (California lilac)

Cistus hybridus and *C.* × *purpureus* (rock rose)

Dianthus deltoides (maiden pink)

Erigeron compositus (fleabane)

Euphorbia × *martinii* (spurge)

Geranium sanguinea and *G.* 'Johnson's Blue'
   (cranesbill)

Helianthemum nummularium (sun rose)

Kniphofia uvaria (redhot poker)

Lantana camara and *L. montevidensis* (lantana)

Lavandula dentata (lavender)

Lupinus arboreus (tree lupine)

Nepeta × *faassenii* (catmint)

Nierembergia spp. (cup flower)

Oenothera speciosa (white evening primrose)

Phlomis fruticosa (Jerusalem sage)

Phormium tenax (New Zealand flax)

Rosmarinus officinalis (rosemary)

Salvia leucantha (Mexican bush sage)

Santolina rosmarinifolia (santolina)

Stachys byzantina (lamb's ears)

Stipa gigantea (giant feather grass)

PLANTED PATHS ARE RELATIVELY CAREFREE

Once installed, our planted paths need very little attention. We feed the plants at planting time with a balanced fertilizer, then twice a year—late winter and early fall—after that. We don't go out of our way to feed the plants in the path, though. Instead, if the path is next to a lawn and we're broadcasting fertilizer on the lawn, we'll broadcast it over the path while we're at it. If the path is next to a perennial border and we're using a diluted liquid fertilizer on the plants in the border, we'll spray the path, too. The point is that we don't need to (and don't want to) fuss over these plants to keep them looking their best. If the weather is dry, a couple of deep waterings a week will keep the planted paths looking healthy and vibrant.

BARBARA BLOSSOM ASHMUN

is a garden designer, writer, and consultant. She is the author of several books, including *Garden Retreats* and *The Garden Design Primer,* and is a contributing editor for *Fine Gardening*.

Perennials *for* Wet Places

Make wet places blaze with color by using plants with striking flowers. Coneflower's pink-purple blossoms grow from summer until frost.

A LANDSCAPER FRIEND and I squished across boggy grass in knee-high rubber boots, surveying my new garden site. "Just turn this lawn into a lake, Barbara," she said. I laughed, but 11 years later, I realize she was right—excavating a lake would have saved me a lot of work. Yet I'm a flower fiend, and I could not imagine sacrificing so much to the smooth surface of water.

Wet spots are common here in Portland, Oregon (USDA Hardiness Zone 8), where we average 36 in. of rain a year. Most of that arrives from November through May. My property sits at the foot of hills and canyons, where it catches winter runoff that streams down the hillsides like so many waterfalls. Even though I've installed underground pipes to carry away surplus water and spent years amending the clay soil to improve the drainage, an inch or more of water collects and stands on the surface of some of my beds and borders for days at a time in winter. But I've discovered plenty of perennials that don't mind getting their feet wet, and my garden is terrifically colorful despite the challenging site.

IRISES EXCEL IN SUNNY, WET SPOTS

One thing I've learned is that you can't go wrong with beardless irises. They thrive in moisture, sending up attractive blades of foliage topped by showy flowers in a wide range of colors. The seasonal show in my sunny, wet spots begins with Siberian iris in midspring and continues—thanks to yellow

Brighten the shade with the blooms of astilbe. The author likes planting masses of astilbe hybrids with different colors and bloom times.

flag, blue flag, Louisiana, and Japanese irises—into early summer.

Siberian irises (*Iris sibirica*), which are hardy to Zone 4, unfurl in May and bloom well into June, transforming my muddy front border into a colorful cottage garden. My favorite cultivar, 'Caesar's Brother', sings out with rich purple flowers. 'Eric the Red', a bright violet-pink Siberian, chimes in, and 'Chilled Wine', a garnet iris suffused with blue, completes the chord.

About the same time, candles of bright yellow flag iris (*Iris pseudacorus*), which thrive to Zone 4, brighten the scene. Their brilliant yellows are a good match for flamboyant red peonies (*Paeonia* spp.) or orange globeflowers (*Trollius chinensis*). The yellow flag's zest to multiply can be overbearing in a border, so I moved them to a drainage ditch at the perimeter of the garden, where they revel in the moisture. A few cultivars—'Roy Davidson', with yellow flowers embellished by brown markings, and 'Holden Clough' with purple markings—are less rambunctious than the species. I also love 'Variegata' for its green- and yellow-striped spring leaves. It too spreads moderately.

What Works where It's Wet

All of the following plants thrive at least as far north as USDA Hardiness Zone 5; most are hardier.

FOR SUN	FOR SHADE
Species irises—except bearded iris hybrids	Astilbes (*Astilbe* spp.)
Daylilies (*Hemerocallis cultivars*)	Meadowsweet (*Filipendula* spp.)
Coneflowers (*Echinacea purpurea*)	Spiderwort (*Tradescantia virginiana*)
Spurge (*Euphorbia palustris*)	Bishops's hat (*Epidmedium* × *versicolor*)
Big betony (*Stachys macrantha*)	European globeflower (*Trollius europaeus*)
Loosestrife (*Lysimachia ciliata*)	Masterwort (*Astrantia major*)
Obedient plant (*Physotegia virginiana*)	Japanese primrose (*Primula japonica*)

Blue flag iris (*Iris versicolor*) also loves damp sites. Its curiously dark leaves are tinged blackish purple at the base, eliciting interest long before the violet-blue flowers open in late spring. 'Gerald Darby' is known for its especially dark stems and deep violet flowers. Blue flag iris is hardy to Zone 3.

Though they're native to the South, Louisiana irises are surprisingly hardy, thriving even in Zone 4. They come in shades of blue, blue-violet, white, purple, yellow, and reddish purple. I grow only one unnamed

"One thing I've learned is that you can't go wrong with beardless irises."

hybrid, a pass-along plant given to me by a friend. Its 2-ft. stems are topped by velvety purple flowers that bloom for weeks in June.

As the Siberian, Louisiana, and flag irises recede, spuria irises (*Iris spuria*), hardy to Zone 5, begin to open, carrying the flag of color into

A good back-of-the-border plant, spuria iris flowers later than most of its relatives. The bright blooms, borne atop stems 3 ft. to 5 ft. tall, carry color into early summer.

In wet shady spots, the airy, off-white plumes of meadowseet shine like a beacon. Its billowy blossoms form a cloud above a cluster of cranesbill (*Geranium endressii*).

DAYLILIES AND CONEFLOWERS BRIGHTEN SUMMER

Daylilies (*Hemerocallis* cvs.) extend the color deeper into summer, with their tight fists of buds opening into yellow, orange, red, cream, and even lavender flowers. They thrive in wet, sunny spots—so well that researchers are experimenting with growing young daylilies hydroponically.

In pastel borders, I'm partial to light yellow 'Frank Hunter' with ruffled, fragrant flowers, and luminous 'Catherine Woodbery', lavender-pink with touches of yellow-green in the throat. To heat up sizzling red and yellow color schemes, I rely on red 'Chicago Brave' and 'Red Orbit'. For small gardens, miniature daylilies are invaluable. I like 'Little Missie', a burgundy beauty with a white edge outlining each petal, and 'Pandora's Box', cream-colored with a striking burgundy eye. The miniatures are also excellent for adding color at the front of summer borders. These cultivars are all hardy to Zone 4.

The blooms of coneflowers (*Echinacea purpurea*), hardy to Zone 3, join the daylilies in July and continue until frost, just as long as you snip off spent flowers. The garden variety is mauve, blending nicely with summer's blue asters (*Aster* × *frikartii*), balloon flowers (*Platycodon grandiflorus*), and speedwell (*Veronica spicata*). But I prefer the more vibrant pink 'Bright Star' coneflower and also enjoy 'White Swan' and 'White Lustre'.

ASTILBES AND MEADOWSWEET BRING COLOR TO DAMP, SHADY SPOTS

It's more challenging to find colorful plants for damp shade but, with some determination, I discovered some sturdy beauties. Astilbes (*Astilbe* spp.) illuminate even the most shadowy of dark places, just as long as

early summer. Spurias have open flowers with narrow petals that flare upward, outward, and downward—the blooms look like gracefully leaping dancers. Colors abound: lavender, yellow, white, purple, maroon-brown, and even magenta. Most of the hybrids are 3 ft. to 5 ft. tall, suitable for the back of the border. I grow some of these tall beauties in front, too, where they break up the monotony of the usual staircase-style arrangement. In the summer, when they go dormant, I cut back the foliage to nearly ground level, and the irises almost disappear as the taller prairie mallows (*Sidalcea malviflora*) and fall-blooming asters (*Aster* spp.) billow out.

The last irises to flower are the Japanese irises (*Iris ensata*), the showiest stars of summer borders. Different cultivars bear colors ranging from violet, purple, magenta, and blue to white and striped. Any is sure to elicit sighs of pleasure. I love the fascinating, white, purple-veined 'Caprician Butterfly'. One perfect flower floating in a bowl of water is enough to make anyone ecstatic. Japanese irises are hardy to Zone 5.

they get plenty of moisture. Plumes of pink, red, peach, white, and lavender flowers gracefully adorn the garden from June through August, depending on the cultivar. I like to swirl all the colors together like a parfait. Astilbe's handsome, ferny foliage is an added attraction before and after bloom period.

Try a variety of selections that bloom in early, middle, and late seasons to thoroughly enjoy astilbes. Some of my favorite *A.* × *arendsii* hybrids are 'Rheinland' and 'Peach Blossom' for early color, and dark red 'Etna' and white 'Bridal Veil' for midseason. For late summer, I like violet-pink *A.* 'Finale' and I certainly couldn't do without the 4-ft.-tall, lavender-pink *A. chinensis* var. *taquetii* 'Superba' for late-season color at the back of the border. All are hardy to Zone 4.

Meadowsweet (*Filipendula* spp.) looks like astilbe's taller cousin, with similarly dissected leaves and plumy flowers. The two go well together. Creamy white *F. ulmaria* blooms like a beacon in late spring, rising 5 ft. tall. Low-growing *F. vulgaris* 'Flore Pleno', with double white flowers atop lacy leaves, attracts attention at the front of damp, shady borders. And for airy elegance, grow 5-ft.-tall *F. rubra* 'Venusta' with opulent pink plumes. These meadowsweets are hardy to Zone 3.

IGNITE THE SHADE WITH CALLA LILIES, GLOBEFLOWER, AND MASTERWORT

The exquisitely shaped calla lily (*Zantedeschia aethiopica*) is probably the flower that's most immortalized by photographers and painters. Each spring, I marvel at the grace of its white, trumpet-shaped flowers and shiny, arrow-shaped leaves. It will grow almost anywhere if you keep it damp. Calla lilies are hardy only to Zone 8, but in colder areas, you can dig up the rhizomes after a frost, clip off the foliage,

and store them in a cool basement over the winter months.

European globeflower (*Trollius europaeus*), hardy to Zone 4, adds a sunny touch to the shade with bright yellow flowers that never fully open, staying furled like a new rose. I love it with blue cranesbill (*Geranium ibericum*) and blue spiderwort (*Tradescantia virginiana*).

Masterwort's (*Astrantia major*) modest charm completely captures my heart. Many small ivory flowers, flushed pink, bloom throughout the summer and fall, wafting sweet scent. Each masterwort blossom is an umbel of tiny flowers, framed by a collar of papery bracts. It's the perfect companion for astilbes, ferns, and hostas and is hardy to Zone 4.

Having grown these plants in heavy clay for 10 years without a bit of fuss or bother, I feel confident recommending them. With so many choices for damp soil, I'm glad I didn't give up and turn my yard into a lake.

The iris family parades its colors from spring to early summer. These Japanese iris hybrids bloom in late spring.

PETER THEVENOT

specializes in espaliered fruit and ornamental trees at his nursery, River Road Farms. He also presents lectures and workshops for professional landscape and nursery associations.

An Espalier for Every Garden

(FAR LEFT) Espaliers command attention in the landscape. This candelabra design serves as the focal point in the author's side garden.

(INSET) Espaliers can be used in untraditional ways. The author trained this Belgian fence to separate his driveway from his side garden.

MY INTEREST IN espalier began when my wife, Beth, and I visited Mount Vernon. I remember being taken by the way the paths in the vegetable garden were lined with plants shaped into low hedges. As I bent down to inspect them, I discovered they were actually espaliered pear trees that bore fruit. On the two walls that bordered the garden, there were more espaliers trained into fan shapes that served as focal points. The way these trees were artfully trained made the garden seem so inviting, while also lending structure and balance to the garden's overall design.

After returning home, I read all the books that I could find on espalier and spent long hours in the hot Tennessee sun with pruning shears in hand, trying to re-create the shapely trees that I had seen at Mount Vernon. Since then I've mastered many designs and even opened a nursery that specializes in espaliered trees. And through the years, I've

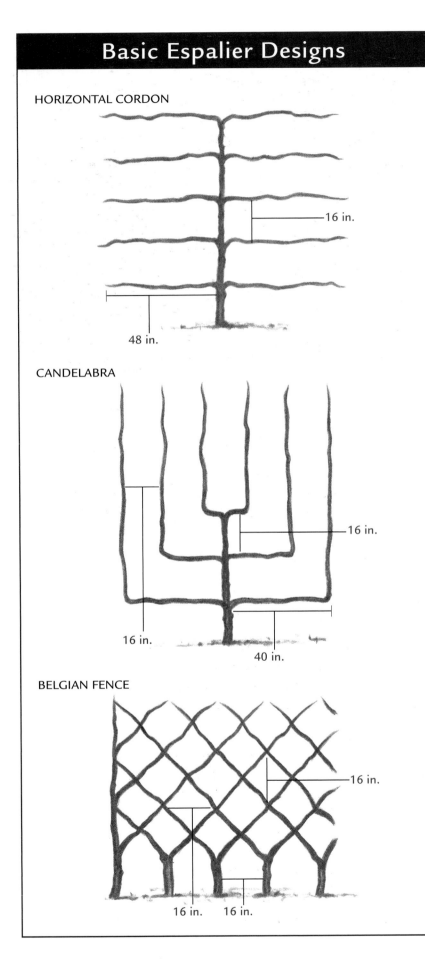

Basic Espalier Designs

HORIZONTAL CORDON

16 in.

48 in.

CANDELABRA

16 in.

16 in.

40 in.

BELGIAN FENCE

16 in.

16 in.   16 in.

learned that all it takes to create beautiful espaliers is a good plan, some judicious pruning, and a little patience.

ESPALIER DESIGNS DICTATE PLACEMENT IN THE GARDEN

There are many different espalier designs, each with a specific use in the garden. The more elaborate designs like the candelabra and the fan are best used as focal points in the garden, while the cordon and the Belgian fence are good for screening views.

The cordon, with its horizontal tiers, is the most common espalier design because it is so versatile. When used as a focal point, cordons typically measure 6 ft. tall by 6 ft. wide, but their design can be modified to fit into any space. The ones trained to the wall in my side garden that serve as a living fence are three-tiered and measure 6 ft. wide by 4 ft. tall. Those at Mount Vernon were made up of one horizontal tier about 3 ft. tall by 8 ft. long.

The candelabra is a more dramatic espalier. Its height and design command attention. One adorns the entryway to our house, and serves as the focal point in our side garden. It is 80 in. wide and stands 8½ ft. tall, which is typical for this design. The space between each branch is 16 in. This spacing may look too wide when the plant is young, but it fills in quickly as the tree matures.

To divide our driveway from our side garden, we planted a Belgian fence. This living wall functions as a see-through screen. Its real interest occurs in winter when its bare branches display its unique shape. Light and air pass through the diamond-shaped gaps in all seasons, and this design blends into our landscape well without seeming as big and bulky as a stone wall or a wooden fence would.

FAST-GROWING TREES ARE GOOD FOR ESPALIER

Originally, espaliers were trained to brick or stone walls because the masonry absorbed the sun's heat and allowed for quick ripening of fruit. This practice evolved in climates not particularly suited to fruit production, such as the monasteries of northern France. Although espaliers are created more for their ornamental value today, the tradition of tethering espaliers to masonry persists for good reason. Brick and stone backdrops require minimal maintenance. When using a painted wooden surface as a backdrop for an espalier, I allow 4 in. to 6 in. between the tree and the wall for maintenance purposes.

Although a number of trees can be espaliered, I prefer the Kieffer pear (*Pyrus* 'Kieffer') for its vigorous growth and lateral habit. Also, it does not require a pollinator to produce fruit, and will usually fruit by its second season. In addition, Kieffer pears have high resistance to disease and are hardy to USDA Hardiness Zone 4. One disadvantage is that their growth hardens fairly quickly, so they require weekly attention during the shaping process.

Other good pear cultivars (*Pyrus* cvs.) for espalier include 'Magnus', 'Bartlett', 'Red Sensation Bartlett', and 'Harrow's Delight'. For apples (*Malus* cvs.), I recommend 'Arkansas Black', 'Red Delicious', 'Golden Delicious', 'Liberty', 'Freedom', and 'Empire'. Good ornamental crabapples (*Malus* cvs.) include 'White Cascade', 'Prairiefire', and 'Golden Raindrops'. Other ornamental plants such as magnolia (*Magnolia grandiflora* 'Little Gem'), rose of Sharon (*Hibiscus syriacus*), and weeping Yaupon holly (*Ilex vomitoria*) can also be espaliered.

You can order whips as bare-root plants or in 1-gallon, 3-gallon, or 5-gallon containers.

These plants should be from 4 ft. to 6 ft. tall. Fruit trees are budded to a variety of different root stocks, each with a number denoting the mature size of the tree. M7, M9, M27, M111 are all good root stocks to use. Ideally, trees with ½-in. to ¾-in. calliper trunks (the thickness at 6 in. above soil level) are best, but smaller-sized trees can be used. Trees for espalier can be purchased at your local nursery or garden center, or ordered from mail-order nurseries.

Since most of the plants I use for espalier produce fruit, I plant them in spaces that receive at least six to eight hours of sunlight, the minimum sun required for proper fruit production. Soil and drainage are also important considerations when I am choosing a site. My espaliers all benefit from southern exposures and well-drained, loamy soil.

Prune espaliers to keep them at the proper height and shape. The author waits until his trees have flowered and set fruit before pruning.

"Although a number of trees can be espaliered, I prefer the Kieffer pear for its vigorous growth and lateral habit."

1 Trace an outline of the espalier design with chalk to use as a guide.

2 Drill holes 2 in. deep with a masonry bit and insert the lag shields.

3 Screw eyebolts into lag shields. The lag shields expand as the bolts are screwed in.

INSTALL A WIRE SUPPORT SYSTEM

Once I've chosen a site, a design to fit the site, and purchased a tree, I use chalk to draw an outline of the espalier design on the surface where I plan to train the tree. This outline measures the exact mature height and width of the design, and serves as a guide when drilling the holes for the eyebolts that hold the guide wires.

Using a masonry bit, I then drill holes at evenly spaced intervals along each tier, usually 16 in. to 24 in. apart. For example, I would drill nine holes spaced 16 in. apart for an 8-ft.-long horizontal tier of a cordon. Each hole should be about 1½ in. to 2 in. deep.

Once the holes are drilled, I place 2-in.-long lag shields into each hole flush with the wall. Lag shields are small metal cylinders with threading that eyebolts screw into. There's a code on most lag shields that tells what size drill bit to use. These lag shields expand and become snug in the wall once the eyebolt is screwed into it. They are only necessary when attaching guide wires to masonry. When training an espalier onto a wooden structure. I screw the eyebolts directly into the wood.

Once the lag shields are in place, I screw in the 6-in.- to 8-in.-long eyebolts, leaving the head of the bolt 4 in. to 6 in. out from the surface of the wall. I then thread 14- or 16-gauge wire through the eye of each bolt several times, being sure to pull the wire tight before threading it through the next eyebolt. These wires will form the structure that the espalier will be trained to and must be taut to support the weight of the tree as it grows. The 4-in. to 6-in. space between the wall and the tree allows for air circulation and prevents fungal and bacterial diseases from plaguing the leaves.

PLANT THE TREE CLOSE TO THE WALL

After getting the guide wires in place, I dig a planting hole twice the size of my tree's root-

4 Thread wire through the eyebolts to form a tight network of guide wires.

5 Position the tree's rootball so that the trunk is about 4 in. from the wall.

6 Attach the trunk to the guide wires with ¼-in. plastic nursery tape.

ball. As I place the rootball into the hole, I line the trunk up with the center vertical wire, placing the trunk as close to the wire as I can get it. If the tree's rootball is too big to allow this, I shave off a few roots on the side facing the wall. The tree should be planted about 4 in. from the wall, with the bud union 2 in. to 3 in. above the soil level.

I then firm the soil around the base of the tree once it is in place, secure the trunk of the tree to the guide wire with ¼-in. nurseryman's tape, and water it well. The ideal time for planting is fall; this gives the root system time to acclimate itself before the growing season begins in spring.

PRUNE THE TREE TO PRODUCE BRANCHES

In late winter or early spring, I cut the top of the tree off to stimulate branch development at about 2 in. above where I want the first tier of branches to emerge. A few days after after I make this cut, small branch buds will start to swell all along the tree's main leader. I then gently rub off all the buds except for the six located closest to the first tier wire.

As these buds start to grow, I select the branch with the most vertical growth habit to become the new main leader (eventually the second tier). I choose two other branches based on their proximity to the guide wires and how straight they are growing to become the first horizontal tier. I don't remove the other three branches until I'm certain that the two I've selected on their way to become tiers.

Sometimes one or more of the six buds I've selected for a tier refuse to grow. In that case, I use a technique called notching to stimulate bud growth. With a sharp knife or pruning-shear blade, I carefully cut a wedge out of the cambium layer of the bark right above the lazy bud. This allows nutrients to pool at the bud notch. When used in early spring, this technique usually triggers buds to grow.

I let the branches grow 6 in. to 8 in. long before bending them to meet the guide wires. If the branches are bent while the wood is still too green, they are likely to break off, and I'll have to start over. I don't worry if the branches are not exactly horizontal because they will straighten out as they grow.

As the branches grow, I gently tie them to the wires at 6-in. to 8-in. intervals. The length of a cordon's tier can vary depending on how much space you have, with some growing horizontally for many feet. The tiers on candelabras, though, need to be bent upward at a certain point to form the vertical sides. I usually make my turns when a branch has grown 6 in. to 8 in. past the location of the desired turn. At that point, I secure the upright part of the branch to the guide wire to keep it growing toward the end of the candelabra's vertical arm. With all espalier designs, when a branch reaches the desired height or length, I simply cut the growing end off and keep the branch pruned to that height or length.

Train and Prune Your Tree into Shape

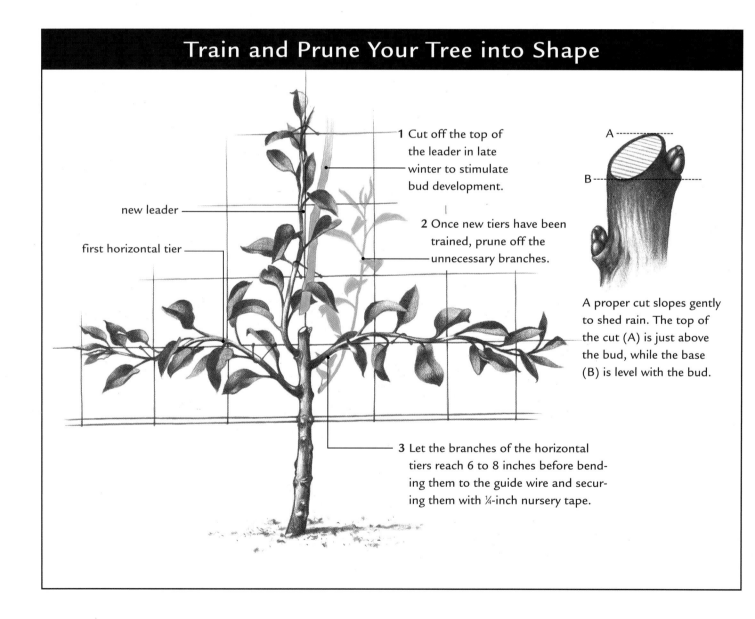

new leader

first horizontal tier

1 Cut off the top of the leader in late winter to stimulate bud development.

2 Once new tiers have been trained, prune off the unnecessary branches.

3 Let the branches of the horizontal tiers reach 6 to 8 inches before bending them to the guide wire and securing them with ¼-inch nursery tape.

A proper cut slopes gently to shed rain. The top of the cut (A) is just above the bud, while the base (B) is level with the bud.

PRUNE REGULARLY TO KEEP ESPALIER SHAPELY

It's important to remember that an espalier is a living sculpture, and it will never be perfect. I like to look at the crooks and turns on my trees as part of their character and charm. The saving grace when practicing this art is that even the most glaring mistakes can be corrected by manipulating new growth.

Since the new growth of the Kieffer pear hardens quickly, it may be possible to miss the opportunity to turn and tie down a branch while it's still flexible. When this happens or when a branch accidentally breaks, I cut the branch back to a nice straight portion at the point of a downward facing bud where a new branch will quickly grow to replace the lost one. When pruning, I always make cuts right above a bud. I stop making cuts 6 to 8 weeks before the first frost is expected. Any new growth stimulated after this point would be susceptible to frost damage.

As the tree continues to grow, side shoots, or spurs, will sprout from the trunk and branches. To keep my espaliers looking neat, tidy, and at the desired height and shape, I prune them back about once a month during the growing season until 6 weeks before the first frost is expected. On trees that produce fruit, I wait until the fruit has set to do any pruning. The optimal length for spurs is 4 in. to 6 in. Pruning the spurs back too short will result in fewer flowers and less fruit.

FERTILIZE AND WATER TO KEEP ESPALIER HEALTHY

To keep my trees looking their best, I diligently water during dry spells, and I feed them once a year in late February or early March with a 180-day time-released balanced fertilizer such as 12-12-12 with micronutrients. I use

Creating a notch into the bark's cambium layer above the dormant bud pools nutrients and stimulates growth.

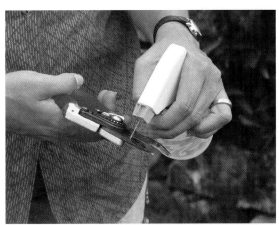

Disinfect pruning shears with alcohol before moving from one tree to the next.

a jeweler's loupe to inspect the leaves of my trees (a magnifying glass would do). Signs of insects such as mites, thrips, aphids, and white flies, as well as the beginnings of fungal and bacterial problems, are hard to spot without magnification. If my scouting uncovers any diseases or insects, I immediately take steps to address the problem.

Patience is a virtue when training trees into espalier. They take some time to grow from gangly whips into the centerpiece of your landscape. Within the first year of growth, their form will start to take shape, but the growth will still be leggy. During the second year, the design becomes recognizable and you might get fruit if you're lucky. It may take up to five years for a tree to reach its desired height, so just rest assured that with each year of growth, your espalier will look better and better.

YEAR-ROUND
INTEREST

4

GARDENS THAT FLOURISH in summer often look deadly in winter. And while there is nothing wrong with creating a garden that peaks in a particular season, it's certainly nice to be able to enjoy our gardens in every season.

The easiest way to create multiseason interest is by adding hardscaping features and evergreens to our gardens. But that's just a beginning. There are many ornamental grasses and perennials whose dried foliage, if left standing, is quite attractive in winter. And there are trees and shrubs that offer colorful foliage in fall, berries in winter, and delightful flowers in spring. In fact, in much of the United States, you can have flowers blooming in your garden year-round. To explore the world of gardening beyond what we normally think of as "the growing season," just turn the page.

Odd Pods & *Sensational* Seed Heads

CAROLE OTTESEN

is the author of four gardening books, including *The Native Plant Primer*. She lectures frequently and serves on the steering committee for the Cullowhee native plants conference.

(FAR LEFT) Strengthen the impact of seed heads by planting in masses. Russet seed heads of *Sedum* 'Autumn Joy' are accented by tawny grasses and a silvery yucca.

(INSET) Seedpods often have striking forms. The long, dark pods of wild senna look like turkey feet. They stand out in front of porcupine grass (*Miscanthus sinensis* 'Strictus').

AS THE BOISTEROUS FLOWERS of summer start going to seed, I welcome what I call the subtle season. Once frosts arrive, all the divergent colors of summer evolve into a muted palette. It's a color harmony unrivaled at any other season—shades of almond, tan, brown, gold, rust, and gray, accented by evergreens. Nature's annual grand finale becomes a tranquil backdrop for eye-catching seed heads and seedpods.

Seeds—the extravagant, intricate handiwork of flowers—continually amaze me. Forged from the fragile stuff of fleeting blossoms, seeds are housed in surprisingly sturdy architecture. These cunning structures crown the garden like sculpture. Many have wondrously odd or elegant shapes.

I'm not alone in my admiration. No sooner do seeds appear than wildlife throngs the garden. Birds, insects, and small mammals descend upon a smorgasbord of seedy

Plants with Seeds of Interest

NAME	HEIGHT	FLOWER	ZONES	CULTURE	LATE-SEASON INTEREST
Abelmoschus manihot aibika	6 ft.	yellow	annual	sun to part shade; ordinary soil	fuzzy, green pods turn tan on tall stems
Achillea filipendulina leaf yarrow	4 ft.	golden-yellow	3–9	sun; well-draining soil	flat, yellow-gray seed fern-heads form excellent texture in masses
Baptisia australis false indigo	4 to 5 ft.	blue-violet	3–9	sun; well-draining soil	dark-purple, bean-like pods
Calamagrostis × *acutiflora* 'Karl Foerster' feather reed grass	4 ft.	white	6–8	sun; ordinary soil	erect, white seed heads; excellent massed
Cassia marilandica wild senna	5 ft.	yellow	4–7	sun; dry soil	black pods resembling turkey feet
Coreopsis verticillata thread-leaved coreopsis	1 to 2 ft.	golden-yellow	4–8	sun; average soil	small, black, beady seed pods hover on clouds of dried foliage
Datura innoxia angel's trumpet	5 to 8 ft.	white	7–10	sun; well-draining soil	spiked, green, mace-like pod
Echinacea spp. coneflowers	3 to 4 ft.	rose-pink, white, magenta	4–9	sun; average to moist soil	round, brown seed heads favored by birds
Helianthus maximilliani Maximillian sunflower	6 to 8 ft.	golden-yellow	4–9	sun; dry soil	dark-tan seed heads arranged along stem; good in bouquets
Lablab purpureus hyacinth bean	6 to 20 ft.	purple	annual	sun; well-draining soil	long, flat pods flushed or entirely purple
Lunaria annua money plant; honesty	2 to 3 ft.	purple, white	5–9	sun to part shade; any soil	white, translucent skin-like disks; good in bouquets
Miscanthus sinensis	6 to 12 ft.	rose	4–9	sun; average soil	satiny, rose plumes turning to tan
Panicum virgatum switch grass	3 to 6 ft.	green	4–9	sun to part shade; any soil	fine, sparkling seeds on threadlike stems
Pennisetum setaceum fountain grass	3 to 4 ft.	pink to purple	6–9	sun; moist soil	foxtail-like seed heads and grass turn almond color after frost
Ricinus communis 'Carmencita' 'Carmencita' castor bean	6 ft.	fuchsia	9–10	sun; moist, warm soil	hairy pods split to reveal patterned seeds
Rudbeckia spp. Black-eyed Susans	2 to 3 ft.	golden with deep brown center	4–8	sun to part shade; ordinary moist soil	dark-brown, cone-shaped seed heads; spectacular massed
Sedum 'Autumn Joy'	2 ft.	reddish-pink	4–8	sun; average soil	dark-copper seed heads; spectacular massed and in bouquets

Hyacinth bean

'Carmencita' castor bean

Fountain grass

Switch grass

delights. It might seem that plants produce these ingenious seedcases and their contents simply for the amusement and benefit of wildlife.

SEEDCASES VARY IN APPEARANCE AND FUNCTION

Besides intriguing my eye and supporting wild creatures, the business of the seeds is deadly earnest. The continuity of each plant species depends on how successfully life is sheltered over winter and conveyed into spring. Plants' vehicles for regeneration enrich the garden with beautiful forms that arise from their function. My delight in each seedcase is enhanced by its solemn purpose. Each shape—long bean, sphere, disk, plume, spike, fat turban, or ball of tightly packed seeds—is a monument to nature's constancy.

Each flowering species has a strategy for survival. Coneflowers (*Echinacea* spp.), confi-

dent that their rhizomatous roots grow ever outward to expand their territory, can afford munificence. They offer up their brown, spiked seed balls freely, inviting birds to feast. And nature's fliers come in flocks, devouring many seeds, but always scattering a few.

Species of *Asclepias*, such as butterfly weed and milkweed, build spacious housing for their numerous progeny. Trusting in amplitude and the wind, their pods curl open long before winter arrives. One by one, over many weeks, seeds on angel-hair wings ride wind currents to a thousand new locations.

The knobby seedpods of false indigo (*Baptisia australis*) resemble those of butterfly weed in size, though not in structure. Less than a dozen large seeds rattle inside a pod, buffeted by winter winds. The hard, leathery shell—which turns dark purple—strains to contain them until, battered and broken, it drops its occupants onto moist spring soil.

False indigo

Aibika

Black-eyed Susan

Angel's trumpet

(ABOVE) The tall seed heads of alliums gleam in summer light.

(RIGHT) As poppy petals drop away, their round seed heads hover above slender stalks.

LEAVE SEEDPODS STANDING OR GATHER FOR ARRANGEMENTS

In purpose and structure, seedpods are more dramatic than flowers. Almost all are longer lasting. These durable vessels are powerful accents in the off-season garden as well as in bouquets.

The earliest seed heads—poppy, allium, and money plant—hint at the riches to come. By late summer, a walk around the garden yields plentiful material for a winter arrangement. I rub off the papery outer skins of money plant (*Lunaria annua*) to reveal the translucent, white centers. Later on, graceful plumes of *Miscanthus* and curling wands of goldenrod (*Solidago* spp.) make frothy fillers. For accents, there are the tight pods of Maximillian sunflower (*Helianthus maximillianii*), the slender seed heads of daylilies (*Hemerocallis* spp.), and the stiff spikes of *Astilbe*.

I'm usually loath to cut other likely candidates for bouquets, as they make splendid tableaux in the garden. The narrow, bumpy, black seedpods of wild senna (*Cassia marilandica*) look like turkey feet and contrast with the soft brilliance of grasses. This combination looks especially lovely when backlit by the setting sun.

The seed balls of angel's trumpets (*Datura innoxia*) make me smile. These feisty members of the deadly nightshade family envelop their seeds in spiky armor. Like miniature medieval maces, they defy predators—including me. I enjoy them, untouched, in the garden—pale-green weapons punctuating a sinuous, leafless snake of stem.

'Carmencita' castor bean (*Ricinus communis* 'Carmencita') is flamboyant in the fall garden with carmine-red pompoms. Resembling hairy baskets, the pods crack open to reveal seeds, wonderfully fat and patterned.

Aibika (*Abelmoschus manihot*) forms elegant, hairy pods that hint at its kinship with okra. Like castor bean and wild senna, this plant in seed is as striking as when its yellow flowers appear.

MASSES ACCENTUATE SEEDS' TEXTURES AND COLORS

I find that one or two yarrow plants in seed look messy. But something wonderful happens when yarrows, especially *Achillea filipendulina*, are massed. Instead of suggesting undone maintenance, their seed heads form a tweedy texture in an appealing yellow-gray.

Massing plants also heightens the impact of their colors in seed. And since the autumnal palette is so compatible I never worry about how plants will combine as they fade. *Sedum* 'Autumn Joy', in its dark-copper fall tone,

functions as an accent beside the less-vivid yarrow seed heads. And while a single *Sedum* 'Autumn Joy' is a good candidate for a dried-flower bouquet, 15 or 20 plants holding their dried seed heads stiffly above dormant plants form a splendid, textural ground cover. To me, this display in my garden outshines my most carefully planned summer border in its absolute perfection of tone.

Always dramatic, the dark-chocolate seed heads of 'Goldsturm' black-eyed Susan (*Rudbeckia fulgida* var. *sullivantii* 'Goldsturm') become riveting when massed in the off-season landscape. Charming as a massed ground cover in summer, tickseed (*Coreopsis verticillata*) and

After clematis flowers fade, the seed heads look like strands of silk.

"Since the autumnal palette is so compatible I never worry about how plants will combine as they fade."

Grass seed heads shimmer in late-afternoon light. The glow of the setting sun illuminates graceful plumes of several grasses.

its cultivars 'Moonbeam' and 'Zagreb' become spectacular in dormancy. The delicate, thread-like foliage, deep green in summer, fades through blends of chartreuse and moss, then darkens to smoky gray. By early winter, the plants hover over the ground like thunder-clouds, studded with hundreds of seed balls like black beads.

"Because light-colored grasses remain supple and voluminous after frost, they're good partners to rigid seed heads."

GRASS SEED HEADS MAKE DAZZLING LIGHT CATCHERS

The seeds of ornamental grasses are most often born in plumes that bring to a garden something unique. Other plants may lend volume, color, and scent. Only grasses enrich gardens with the quality of dazzle. They capture the brilliance of light and display it in their seed heads.

Big grasses such as *Miscanthus sinensis* and its cultivars bear dozens of plumes. Like torches, light-catching plumes of grasses can be sited to guide a visitor through a garden. Or they can stand at the edge of the garden, effectively stopping the eye.

Smaller grasses such as *Miscanthus sinensis* var. *purpurascens* or feather reed grass (*Calamagrostis* × *acutiflora* 'Karl Foerster') planted throughout the borders create a leitmotiv of dazzling light. Even more subtle in effect, the shiny seeds of switch grass (*Panicum virgatum*) are held above the plants on ethereal stems. Like tiny diamonds, these seeds glisten and reflect late-season light.

DESIGN PAIRINGS TO ACCENT SEASONAL CHANGES

Ornamental grasses are some of the most cooperative plants to include when designing with seed heads in mind. Most are dormant in early spring, which makes them ideal companions for bulbs. They come into fullness in high summer and usually wait until fall to produce their plumes. Frost blanches their foliage to shades of almond and tan to make them wonderful complements, certainly to evergreens, but also to the grays, browns, russets, and tans of other fading perennials.

Design for late-season contrast by juxtaposing textures and habits. For example, because light-colored grasses remain supple and voluminous after frost, they're good partners to rigid seed heads, which are often hoisted on dry, spindly stems. A tall, cream-colored *Miscanthus sinensis* surrounded by a sea of brown-black seed heads of 'Goldsturm' black-eyed Susan is the splendid and long-lasting culmination of two eminently suitable partners. While black-eyed Susan's spiky seed heads stand stiff, the almond-colored, papery grass blades sway and whisper in the wind. This partnership begins in late spring when both grass and perennial leaves appear at precisely the right moment to gracefully camouflage the foliage of spent spring bulbs. In sum-

Peel the soft coating of money plant's seedpods to reveal translucent white disks. They look appealing in dried arrangements.

mer, the pair comes into voluptuous maturity in tandem.

Plan borders to highlight spectacular seeds. Site tall accents like aibika in a sea of feather reed grass. Or plant *Crocosmia masoniorum* 'Lucifer' behind a mass of yarrow that is edged with tickseed for vibrant summer blooms and a late-season spectacle. Experiment freely. Choose plants for their distinctive seeds and work backward to spring planting. At the very least, you know you'll get the late season right.

Plants gone to seed often create winter interest, like the ice crusts around the seed heads of these 'Goldsturm' black-eyed Susans.

Scented Shrubs *for All* Seasons

ERICA GLASENER

is a contributing editor for *Fine Gardening* and the host of HGTV's *A Gardener's Diary*. Previously she was in charge of the educational program at the Scott Arboretum of Swarthmore College.

Surround yourself with scent by placing benches amid fragrant plants. This intimate sunken garden helps to contain the delicate springtime aroma of daphne.

OR ME, THE SENSE OF SMELL has great power to bring back memories and transport me into the past. I will always think of my grandmother's garden whenever I get a whiff of gardenias, and when I sniff the intoxicating scent of lilacs, I think of spring at Swarthmore College (home of the Scott Arboretum) when classes were held in the middle of the lilac collection.

When you grow plants with fragrant flowers or aromatic foliage, your garden becomes a retreat from the outside world, an oasis that offers not only visual beauty, but also scented pleasures for every season. Scented plants and flowers have long been grown for their therapeutic and often intoxicating effects—sensations that were lauded by poets such as Francis Bacon. Even in the 16th century, it was known that scent in flowers comes from volatile oils, which are located in the petals and released into the air naturally. In leaves, these oils are located deep below the

A less demanding daphne, 'Carol Mackie' provides beautifully variegated semievergreen foliage as well as fragrance.

One blossom can perfume an entire room. Sweet shrub starts to flower as early as May and often continues through June and July.

"If your garden space is limited, many fragrant plants will grow happily in containers."

surface, and the leaves must be bruised or crushed in order to release their scents.

Over the years, I have discovered some choice fragrant shrubs that are ornamental as well as fragrant.

DESIGNING FOR PLEASURES OF THE NOSE

When I recommend shrubs for home gardeners, I consider not only bloom, texture and form, but also the presence of pleasing scent. If you plan carefully, your garden can offer delightful fragrances year-round.

Make sure to place fragrant plants where they will be most appreciated. Courtyards or enclosed spaces help trap scents and encourage them to linger. Reserve areas near entryways and along paths for plants with aromatic leaves that will give up their sweetness when you brush against them. Don't forget to include a bench or strategically placed chairs where you can sit and enjoy your garden and its many fragrances.

Plant hardy shrubs in combination with sweet-smelling herbs, annuals and perennials to obtain maximum olfactory pleasure. If your garden space is limited, many fragrant plants will grow happily in containers; this way, you can easily move them into the spotlight when they are at their peak of scent.

Keep in mind, too, that the scent of many flowers varies according to the temperature and time of day. I remember driving with a friend, our windows rolled down to catch the warm, humid spring air, when we were so overwhelmed by a strong strawberrylike smell that my friend stopped the car so we could investigate. The source turned out to be a plant called sweet shrub in bloom in someone's yard more than 100 ft. away! On a cooler day, we probably wouldn't have noticed this plant.

SOME SCENTED SHRUBS ARE DECIDUOUS

The sweet shrub (*Calycanthus floridus*) we discovered on our drive is an old-time favorite cultivated for more than 200 years. It's known by a variety of regional common names including Carolina allspice and strawberry shrub. Native from Virginia to Florida, it blooms in May and continues on and off into June and July.

Hardy from USDA Hardiness Zones 4 to 9, this trouble-free deciduous shrub can look straggly in the wild, but in the garden it has a dense, rounded habit—growing 6 ft. to 9 ft. tall and as wide. Sweet shrub adapts to many soil types and grows in sun or shade, but I have noticed more blooms when it is grown in full sun. There is also a cultivar with pale yellow to yellow-green flowers, but to my taste the species is superior.

Composed of many copper or reddish brown petals, the flowers smell like straw-

Add a little native spice to the garden. Summersweet seasons the late summer air with its clove-scented flowers.

berries or a combination of strawberries, banana and pineapple—just one can perfume an entire room. Sweet shrub also has aromatic foliage and bark. Do your own sniff test before you purchase this shrub, or make sure that you are getting a variety known for its fragrance.

A good evergreen ground cover underneath sweet shrub is sweet box (*Sarcococca hookeriana* var. *humilis*). Sweet box forms a glossy carpet with an early spring bloom of inconspicuous but sweetly fragrant flowers.

"Daphnes are at the top of my list for their sweetly scented flowers."

Inconspicuous but fragrant, the flowers of sweet box, an evergreen ground cover, appear in early spring. Plant it underneath sweet shrub for maximum olfactory impact.

A late bloomer, thorny elaeagnus is tolerant of many adverse growing situations. Its gardenia-like perfume wafts through the air in autumn.

A shrub that extends the season of bloom beyond spring is called summersweet or sweet pepperbush (*Clethra alnifolia*). Native from Maine to Florida, it often spreads by suckers to form thickets in the wild. Reserve a spot in the shrub border or a woodland garden for this choice deciduous shrub.

Its white, deliciously spicy clove-scented flowers appear on upright panicles that last four to six weeks in July and August. Two cultivars, 'Rosea' and 'Pink Spire', have pink-tinted flowers. The leaves start out a lustrous deep green and turn to yellow and gold in the fall. Hardy from Zones 3 to 9, it is oval or upright and erect in habit, ranging from 3 ft. to 8 ft. tall and 4 ft. to 5 ft. wide, depending on where it is growing.

This pest-free native tolerates wet soils as well as dry conditions and will grow in shade or sun. Summersweet is also a favorite of bees. *Clethra alnifolia* 'Hummingbird' is a relatively new cultivar that is well suited for small gardens, growing 3 ft. tall and wide at maturity.

I think of mock orange (*Philadelphus coronarius*) as an old-fashioned favorite—a pass-along plant sometimes found in old, abandoned gardens. Its common name is inspired by the sweet, citrusy scent of the flowers that appear in May to early June.

Hardy from Zones 4 to 8, mock orange is a large deciduous shrub, growing 10 ft. to 12 ft. tall and as wide. It looks best intermixed with other shrubs or at the back of a border with spring-blooming perennials. Adaptable to full sun or light shade, it prefers a moist, well-drained soil. There are numerous hybrids and cultivars that are listed as having fragrant flowers.

MANY EVERGREENS ARE ALSO FRAGRANT

Despite their reputation for being difficult to grow, daphnes are at the top of my list for their sweetly scented flowers. Good drainage is essential, and even then, daphnes may suffer from leaf spot, twig dieback, canker, virus or what I call the "daphne death dance," where they appear to die overnight for no reason. Of the daphnes that I have successfully grown, two appear to be less finicky and offer delightful fragrant flowers.

Daphne × *burkwoodii* 'Carol Mackie', a semievergreen shrub growing to 3 ft. tall and at least as wide, is hardy from Zones 4 to 8. The light pink flowers have a delicate, sweet fragrance that is best appreciated at close range. Flowers appear in clusters at the ends of branches in May. Even when this variegated selection is not blooming, it makes a lovely mounded shrub. Its delicate green foliage has margins edged in cream.

One of the parents of *D.* × *burkwoodii* is *D. caucasica*, a deciduous daphne hardy from Zones 6 to 8. This small to medium-size plant matures at 4 ft. to 5 ft. high and wide, and produces masses of tiny but powerfully scented white flowers in May and June, and continues blooming on and off through summer.

Thorny elaeagnus (*Elaeagnus pungens*) is an evergreen shrub that elicits strong comments from gardeners. Considered a weed by some, this shrub thrives in the sun or shade and in all types of soil. It is impervious to pests, pollution and salt spray, making it an ideal candidate for hedges, screening and bank plantings.

During October and November, its flowers provide a delightful gardenialike perfume. The flowers are often hidden by the handsome foliage—tough and lustrous green above, dull and silvery dotted with brown below.

Hardy to Zone 6, this aggressive grower is not for the small garden, reaching 10 ft. to 15 ft. tall and as wide in no time at all. The best way to use thorny elaeagnus is to take the long shoots it produces and train them up over an arbor or trellis.

SELECT BY SCENT APPEAL

The perception of a particular scent varies from nose to nose—I'd describe gardenia as pleasantly heady while someone else might find it overwhelming. To help determine your favorite smells, pinch a leaf and crush it, or cut a blossom and bring it into the house. The best way to select the right scents for your garden is to visit nurseries when the fragrant plants are in bloom, and at different times of day, since scents vary with the weather.

Scented schrubs can add charm to your garden and create an atmosphere that is not only beautiful but also filled with scents throughout the year.

An old-fashioned favorite whose name is inspired by its citrus-scented flowers, mock orange blooms in late spring.

NANCY BRITZ

specializes in daylilies and conifers. Her garden has been featured on the Garden Conservancy and Tour, and is an official display garden of the American Hemerocallis Society.

Composing with Conifers

A garden composed largely of conifers provides year-round interest. Different shapes and colors contrast for a dynamic look.

WHEN MY HUSBAND and I built a new house filled with large windows, I wanted beautiful views all year-round. Perennial borders were my first choice, until I remembered that they require intensive maintenance and that they often fall far short of gorgeous during the winter. Then I thought of conifers—they don't need much care, they're hardy, and they look beautiful no matter what the season. Even in the bleakest winter, the garden looks like a garden—thanks to these evergreens.

Since then, I have discovered that evergreen conifers can be useful in almost any garden design. I find them unexcelled as privacy screens or foundation plantings, as backgrounds for flower borders, as specimens, and as accents in the smallest rock gardens or at the edge of vast forests.

By the time I moved to an old-fashioned farmhouse in Hamilton, Massachusetts, six years ago, I liked conifers enough to dig as many as I could from the old house in New

Billowing grass-
es soften conif-
erous plantings.

Conifers of all shapes and
sizes grow in raised beds
that can be seen from the
house.

Contrast shapes, placing
conical or cylindrical conifers
next to those with mounded
or spreading forms.

Vary the color among
conifers, using gold
or blue for accent.

York and deliver them to my new home near
Boston. After piloting nine large truckloads of
evergreens across southern New England, I
could hardly wait to begin planting a new garden, one that would incorporate everything I
had learned about designing with conifers.

CHOOSE CONIFERS THAT FIT THE SCALE OF THE GARDEN

The first step in creating a conifer-rich planting is deciding how big to make the garden.
That done, I select conifers to complement
its size. Small gardens or rock gardens work
with small, slow-growing, dwarf or miniature
trees. Larger gardens can accommodate
intermediate-sized or large trees.

That said, I never allow a garden's size to be
the sole determining factor in selecting plants.
I also consider the role the planting will play.
A wide privacy screen requires large trees,
even if the planting area is relatively small.
And in even the biggest rock gardens, a full-
sized tree looks out of place.

Since I am unable to resist the attractions of
all kinds of conifers, I decided to create two
separate plantings, each on a scale of its own.
One would be a big, semicircular bed with
large evergreens—white pines, Norway spruce,
Frasier firs—standing at the back of the bed to
serve as a screen along my property line and
to create a background for intermediate-sized

conifers planted in front. For the smaller garden, I planned an array of free-form, raised beds planted with miniature and dwarf conifers, as well as ground-hugging perennials. Curving paths would thread between the smaller beds, making it easier to view the plants.

SILHOUETTES DEFINE A CONIFER'S SHAPE

After deciding what size conifers to use, I had to start thinking about using them in combination with each other. Doing it well can be difficult; conifer colors are subtle, and their shapes never really change. A conifer shaped like a Christmas tree looks like a cone whether it's 5 years old or 50 years old.

For a designer, those unchanging shapes are both charming and challenging. The trick is turning those static forms into dynamic compositions. It's almost like creating a sculpture. For me, the whole secret lies in juxtaposing shapes so that the individuality of each tree or shrub is accentuated by its nearest neighbors.

That's not as difficult as it sounds. It's just a matter of mixing shapes. And luckily, nearly all conifers take one of four basic shapes. Except for weeping varieties and a few irregular cultivars, most conifers can be roughly classed as flat, round, conical, or cylindrical. "Roughly" is the key word; I always allow for some variation. But for simplicity's sake, I still think of both a ball-shaped false cypress and a moundlike 'Blue Star' juniper as being basically round.

To make understanding the shapes even simpler, I find it useful to think of them as silhouettes. Then I need consider only the straight or curved lines that define their margins. If the plant's lines are horizontal, it's a flat, ground-hugging variety, such as a 'Blue Carpet' juniper. If they are upright and nearly

parallel, the tree is a cylinder, like a 'Moonglow' juniper. If the lines form an upside-down "V" and are simply a pair of slanted straight lines, it's a cone-shaped tree, one that looks like a Christmas tree. Finally, if the silhouette is composed of curved lines that form a circle or oval, the conifer is one of the round varieties, like a 'Montgomery' blue spruce. Once you understand the shapes, making eye-catching combinations is easy.

BLEND SIZES AND SHAPES TO CREATE VISUAL INTEREST

To me, a successful planting of conifers is like the skyline of a great city—a creative, eye-pleasing blend of varied sizes and shapes. Close-up views reveal the essence of an indi-

Add color for accent. A bronzy *Thuja occidentalis* 'Sudworthii' brightens hinoki cypress (*Chamaecyparis obtusa* 'Nana Gracilis'), at lower left, and 'Moonglow' juniper (*Juniperus scopulorum* 'Moonglow'), right.

Conifers by Shape, Color, and Size

Conifers come in four basic shapes: round (or mounded); flat, ground-hugging; conical; and cylindrical. Combining those shapes to heighten the contrast between them creates dynamic compositions in the garden. Greater effects are possible when conifer color variations—ranging from golden-yellow to silvery-blue—are incorporated in a grouping of plants. At the right, the author names some of her favorite cultivars.

The strong contrasts of shape and color can be effective, but it is best to avoid extremes in the size of adjacent plants. Conifers exhibit four distinct growth habits: miniature, dwarf, intermediate-sized, and large. Growth patterns are usually found on the plant's nursery tag. Miniatures grow no more than 3 in. a year and reach a maximum height of 3 ft. within 10 years. Dwarfs grow up to 6 in. in a season, and in 10 years reach a height between 3 ft. and 6 ft. Intermediates grow up to a foot a year and, in a decade, top out at somewhere between 6 ft. and 15 ft. Large conifers grow a foot or more a year and reach heights in excess of 15 ft. in 10 years. These are rough guidelines, since growth rates are greatly affected by your USDA Hardiness Zone, microclimate, soil, and growing conditions.

Mounded and round

Conical

Cylindrical

vidual tree or building by baring its shape, color, and texture. But when seen from a distance, the colors and textures fade. Shapes dominate. And those contrasting shapes are what provide the drama and sense of wonder I so often experience when viewing a majestic city skyline—or a great planting of conifers.

Just as buildings are the architectural building blocks of a city, conifers are the structural backbone of a garden. And because the view

COMBINE CONIFERS FOR MAXIMUM CONTRAST

My guiding design principle for combining those shapes is to seek maximum contrast. For me, the most vivid and pleasing picture results when no two similar shapes are placed next to one another. I like to work with small groupings, and take care to make each conifer as different as possible from its neighbors. One of my favorite compositions, for example, began with a 'Montgomery' blue spruce (*Picea pungens* 'Montgomery'), one of the round conifers. I wanted to place something cone-shaped next to it, so I added the broadly conical hinoki cypress (*Chamaecyparis obtusa* 'Nana Lutea'). Then, to maximize the contrast, I planted a flat, ground-hugging 'Nana' Japanese juniper (*Juniperus procumbens*

Perennials can be used to fill out young plantings. The fluffy seed heads of pasque flower also add seasonal interest to this grouping of conifers.

of a conifer bed is usually a "skyline" view—they are often seen from a distance—shape is my primary consideration when designing a new planting.

"The whole secret lies in juxtaposing shapes so that the individuality of each tree or shrub is accentuated by its nearest neighbors."

To make sure I'll like a combination, I experiment before planting. Since conifers usually come from the nursery in containers or balled and burlapped, it's easy to arrange and rearrange them—even at the nursery.

Size is the one characteristic to keep more or less consistent in a conifer planting. You don't want to plant a 12-in.-tall miniature next to something that will grow to a height of 50 ft. or more. Still, you can mix and match a little. In small planting beds, I use mainly miniatures and dwarfs, but I've discovered that intermediate-sized ground-huggers or slim cylinders serve well as accents because they never get too massive.

FILL OUT A BED OF CONIFERS WITH PERENNIALS

When planting, I'm always careful to leave plenty of room between each conifer. Generous spacing eliminates the need to move a crowded conifer after a few years. More space also allows better air circulation and thus promotes healthier growth. The most important reason for generous spacing, however, is aesthetic. I think the beauty of a conifer's shape is diminished if nearby plants obscure their silhouettes.

But, if the new plantings are properly spaced, the garden may look rather sparse. I use perennials to fill some of the empty spaces and to contribute extra color. I especially like vigorous ground-huggers, since they don't intrude on the conifers' more lofty domain. High on my list is almost any thyme. I also like *Gypsophila repens*, a mat forming relative of baby's breath, which comes in pink or white.

A few taller accent plants complement rather than compete with conifers. Among my favorites are pasque flowers (*Pulsatilla vulgaris*), whose extra-early blooms come in white,

Ground-hugging conifers are a perfect partner for more upright varieties. The sprawling *Juniperus procumbens* 'Nana' fronts a *Chamaecyparis obtusa* 'Nana Lutea' and a steely-blue *Picea pungens* 'Montgomery'.

'Nana'). For a more vertical composition, I could have used a cylinder-shaped conifer instead.

I like to maximize contrast in conifer groupings by also varying the colors of each adjoining conifer. Many are available in three or four shades each of green, blue, and yellow. I also consider more elusive qualities, such as the texture of the foliage and the habit of the conifer. Some are airy and open, for example, while others are dense and compact.

CONIFERS SHINE THROUGH FOUR SEASONS

Conifers are the kings of all foliage plants, no matter what the season. In spring, the colors of their new growth seem extra rich because there are few flowers to compete. Later, they provide a backdrop for splashy, summer blooms. Conifer colors take on a renewed glow in fall, when their greens, blues, and yellows contrast marvelously with autumn reds and yellows. Even in the dead of winter, conifers shine. Lightly etched with a dusting of powder or bent under wet snow, the fairyland created by their wonderful shapes enlivens the short, dark days. I am amazed, year after year, at the way conifers seduce me in each new season.

Mix shapes, sizes, and colors to enliven a collection of conifers. A bright yellow *Chamaecyparis obtusa* 'Crippsii' shines in a stand of trees that includes the tall, cylinder-shaped *Juniperus scopulorum* 'Skyrocket' and the conical Alberta spruce.

purple, or wine. They have long-lasting, fluffy seed heads and lacy foliage that remains attractive until frost. Near all but the tiniest conifers, *Sedum* 'Autumn Joy' and dwarf fountain grass (*Pennisetum alopecuroides* 'Hameln') make enhancing, not overpowering, companions.

"I think the beauty of a conifer's shape is diminished if nearby plants obscure their silhouettes."

KEN TWOMBLY

is the owner of Twombly Nursery, which specializes in hard-to-find trees, conifers, and shrubs and offers educational programs featuring nationally known speakers.

Make Winter *a* Wonderland

Peeling bark has eye appeal. The cinnamon-colored sheets of bark peeling off this 'Heritage' river birch never fail to attract attention.

I DIDN'T KNOW BEANS about winter gardens when I first laid eyes on one. During a February botanic tour to Great Britain, I marveled at the extensive plantings of heaths, heathers, and the like displayed for their winter beauty. But, attractive as they were, I thought there was a big flaw in the gardens I saw—there were no interesting contours, no sturdy-looking, structural woody plants, no focal points. They were just masses of plants. I thought I could do better.

Not being one to rush into things, I contemplated the idea for a couple years. The more I considered the possibilities, the more intrigued I became. I thought about creating a landscape of gentle berms and swales bisected by a rocky stream bed. I'd place lots of old, lichened stone about the site, then create a series of beds and borders filled with colorful, sculptural-looking trees, shrubs, and perennials selected especially for their winter beauty.

139

(ABOVE LEFT) Red berries radiate against a blanket of snow. The berries of 'Winter King' hawthorn are especially eye-catching.

(ABOVE RIGHT) Yellow makes green more vivid. The contrast it provides makes yellow winter's most important color. Evergreen perennials accent woody plants any time of year.

As a garden designer and nursery owner, I had both the land and the raw materials to develop a sizable garden, but you could easily make a wonderful winter display in a small area. I often tell customers to pick a spot outside their kitchen window and create a winter garden with something as simple as a bronzy-leaved rhododendron—*Rhododendron* 'PJM Elite', *R.* 'PJM Regal', and *R.* 'PJM Compacta' are some of my favorites—and a few red- and yellow-twig dogwoods (*Cornus stolonifera* 'Cardinal' and *C. s.* 'Flaviramea'). No matter what scale you work on, the key is creating strong contrasts. It's not like gardening in summer when you can use subtle foliage effects or gentle color groupings. In winter, you have to be bold.

BEGIN WITH A BACKBONE OF SCULPTURAL PLANTS

I've never been the kind of gardener who could create a plan on paper and then go out and implement it. I like to make decisions in the field and, if necessary, move things around

after they've been planted. As far as I'm concerned, design mistakes just give me the chance to do more gardening. That said, I did have to make some firm decisions about creating my winter garden. I wanted to take advantage of the natural contours of the land and to echo their curving shapes in the paths and beds. I also brought in lots of stones and used them to create seats, bridges, and small lookouts throughout the garden. To me, stones look wonderfully elemental in a winter landscape, and their enduring structure brings a sense of cohesion to my overall design.

Another important element for a winter garden is a dark, solid-looking background. I was able to take advantage of a hedge of conifers and some big rhododendrons that were already in place in my garden and used them as a backdrop against which the structural forms, naked branches, bright berries, and colored bark of the plants would shine. Stone walls could work, too.

With the site prepared, I began selecting the largest trees and shrubs. This included a good variety of conifers selected for their varied sizes, shapes, and color; deciduous trees selected for their interesting bark, pleasing branching structure, or appealing growth habit; and anything with berries or ornamental fruits. I added a number of weeping trees, too—I've learned that their unusual, striking shapes have an unequaled capacity to surprise garden visitors.

Though I like plants with unique character, they don't have to be exotic. Some of my best specimens were common plants with missing branches or twisted trunks that no one would buy at my nursery. I planted some of these misshapen specimens at a tilt to provide even more interest.

I started putting all these elements together, always opting for maximum contrast. To me, there's nothing as effective as placing a nee-

"To me, stones look wonderfully elemental in a winter landscape..."

dled conifer next to a broadleaved evergreen next to a naked twig next to a berried branch. I try to mix shapes, too, combining mounding forms with upright, spreading, or weeping ones. Texture is another quality to vary. I like to create visual tension by placing, say, a stiff, steely blue spruce next to a soft-looking pine. Size is another good element to play with, and when combining different-size plants, I think in terms of thirds—positioning a large tree next to something that is a third or two-thirds as big.

Here, golden sword yucca complements an 'Aurea' Scots pine.

I also love to plant trees and shrubs in groups to create a lot of impact and to show off the appealing characteristics of the plants. So my garden includes clusters of contorted filberts (*Corylus avellana* 'Pendula') and groupings of mountain clethra (*Clethra acuminata*) and golden curly willows (*Salix* 'Golden Curls'). When making groupings, I strive for compositions based on odd numbers, but I sometimes include a stone as one of the compositional elements. One of the keys to using woody plants is placing them at natural focal points in the garden. To find these spots, I walk around the garden, considering the twists and turns of the paths and noting the way my eye moves across the landscape.

ADD COLOR WITH BARK, BERRIES, AND EVERGREENS

Because deciduous trees are stripped of their leaves in winter, the best candidates for winter gardens have peeling or colorful bark or branches weighted with colorful berries. I especially like the cinnamon-colored sheets of bark peeling off a river birch (*Betula nigra* 'Heritage'), or the darker, curling tissue that unreels from the trunk of a paperbark maple (*Acer griseum*). The mottled bark of Japanese red pine (*Pinus densiflora*) is always a standout. The reddish, peeling bark of climbing hydrangea (*Hydrangea anomala* ssp. *petiolaris*) is a show-stopper, too; I like to let this shade-loving vine scramble along a stone wall. For color, it's hard to beat the red- and yellow-twig dogwoods, whose young branches turn rich shades of those colors in winter. I especially like the cultivar 'Cardinal'—its bark goes from red to yellow and back again as the seasons change. I also like the bold red branches of Japanese maples (*Acer palmatum*) like 'Sango-Kaku' or 'Beni-Kawa', and the squiggly, yellow or red curlicues of curly willow.

Garden ornaments and hardscaping features can add form to the winter garden.

Evergreen trees and shrubs offer a solid mass of color in the winter garden.

When the leaves have fallen, a deciduous tree's branching form offers interest.

Seek out yellow or red bark, berries, and grasses for splashes of color.

Warm up cool scenes with flowering shrubs. Witch hazels, such as this 'Arnold Promise', provide reliable winter blooms.

For fruit-bearing shrubs, I'm partial to crabapples (*Malus* spp.) and winterberry, especially *Ilex verticillata* 'Winter Red' and *I.* 'Sparkleberry'—both look great against an evergreen backdrop. They'll also need a male plant nearby to pollinate the flowers or there won't be any berries. For a berried, ground-covering shrub, I'm particularly fond of willowleaf cotoneaster (*Cotoneaster salicifolius* 'Repens'); it holds its leaves and berries through the whole winter.

Getting the most visual impact from bark or berries can be a little tricky. Without a contrasting background, they won't stand out very well. I like to place plants with berries or colorful bark against an evergreen background, either a hedge or a large specimen. Even a single spray of berries can look magnificent against the shiny, steely needles of a blue spruce. And, coated with a light blanket of snow, woodies with dec-orative bark or clusters of berries take on a whole new dimension of beauty.

Any winter garden should include lots of evergreen conifers. But I think a garden composed solely of evergreen conifers is boring—there's just not enough variety throughout the seasons. So I mix the conifers with deciduous trees or broadleaved evergreens with green or bronzy winter color.

It's also important to vary the color, shape, and texture of conifers in the garden. There are blues, greens, and golds, and all kinds of shapes and sizes. There's enormous variety in their textures—white pines look soft; spruces look stiff; and false cypresses have an almost layered, flowing quality. They can be combined in hundreds of effective partnerships, as long as you maintain a sense of scale. A 100-ft.-tall spruce would make an 18-in. dwarf false cypress look kind of silly if the two were planted side by side.

To me, the most important color in designing a winter garden is yellow—you can't appreciate green without a contrasting touch of yellow. And there are plenty of yellow or gold conifers to choose from. One of my favorites is the dragon's eye pine (*Pinus densiflora* 'Oculis Draconis')—its variegated needles combine both colors. I've also made a few successful yellow-on-yellow plantings by pairing the spiky, bare branches of a yellow-twig dogwood with a Hinoki cypress (*Chamaecyparis obtusa* 'Crippsii'), which, to me, is the aristocrat of yellow conifers.

USE PERENNIALS AS ACCENTS

Though woody plants are the heart and soul of my winter garden, I make use of a wide range of perennials. But I chose them for the way they look in winter, even if they're dormant during the coldest months of the year. A

"To me, the most important color in designing a winter garden is yellow."

plant's structure and foliage are far more important in the winter garden. Whatever perennials I use, they are almost always planted near the outer boundary of a border or bed. To me, they're edging plants. All the woodies give the winter garden a bigger-than-life feel, and in that scale, the perennials, even big ones, seem rather small and decorative by comparison.

Few gardeners grow perennials for the way they look in winter, but there are many plants with terrific presence that time of year. The bright bayonets of a golden sword yucca (*Yucca filamentosa* 'Golden Sword') make a fine foil for a pine (*Pinus sylvestris* 'Aurea'), with a bronze color in winter, or a stand of red-twig dogwoods. Euphorbias are also an effective winter perennial—many varieties have an excellent aboveground presence throughout the year. I like the deep purple leaves of spurge (*Euphorbia amygdaloides* 'Purpurea') in my USDA Hardiness Zone 6 garden; they look especially striking next to the honey-colored, winter-blooming flowers of witch hazel (*Hamamelis* × *intermedia* 'Arnold Promise'). Witch hazel provides its own garden intrigue in winter, when snows coat its yellow blossoms.

Then of course, there are the grasses. Nearly all the perennial grasses have good winter interest, with soft textures and seed heads that wave in the wind like banners. Nearly any miscanthus (*Miscanthus* spp.) or fountain grass (*Pennisetum* spp.) can find useful employment in a planting scheme. Heaths (*Erica* spp.) and heathers (*Calluna* spp.) are other good choices, especially any of the brightly colored cultivars.

When snow flies, the dried stalks of Sedum 'Autumn Joy' create a silhouette that looks especially intriguing, even more so if the composition includes the graceful shapes created by the trunk and branches of a Japanese maple.

SIT BACK AND ENJOY IT ALL WINTER LONG

In spring, summer, and fall, I sometimes work at redesigning parts of the winter garden. I think of it as an ongoing process that will never be finished. Right now I'm working to add maximum interest to my garden in summer and fall.

One of the real delights of a winter garden is that during the season when the garden shines brightest, there's virtually nothing to do in the way of maintenance. There's no watering, no weeding, and no deadheading. All you have to do is look out the window and enjoy it.

Red acts like a beacon in winter. The branches of this 'Sango-Kaku' Japanese maple turn scarlet in fall.

NANCY GOODWIN

is recognized for introducing many species of cyclamen and other perennials to American gardens and has received numerous awards from the horticulture industry.

Fill
Winter
with
Flowers

(CLOCKWISE FROM TOP LEFT) *Crocus tommasinianus, Galanthus elwesii, Helleborus niger,* and *Cyclamen coum* flower while most perennials are dormant.

IN WINTER I SEE the shape of my garden. Paths, fences, and stone walls emerge from their summer blankets of bloom to stand alone and exposed in a landscape shorn of color. In this austere landscape, flowers are more precious to me than jewels. I've been searching for winter-blooming plants for years, and have discovered many that bloom in this, the coldest of seasons. Today at Montrose, my garden in Hillsborough, North Carolina, there is bloom every day of the year.

A HELLEBORE MARKS THE SEASON'S START

Winter begins shortly after Thanksgiving, when *Helleborus vesicarius* revives. I always worry about plants that go dormant and disappear in summer, so I rejoice each year at the sight of its emerging shoots. Large, shiny, dark green leaves grow to about 5 in. above the ground, followed in January or February by up-facing, green, cup-shaped flowers with burgundy markings inside and out.

Helleborus orientalis hybrids bloom beginning in July in a woodland garden.

Some are as large as 4 in. in diameter, while others are as small as an inch and a half across. *H.n.* ssp. *macranthus*, one of my favorites, holds its dark green leaves well above the flowers, hiding them, but also protecting them from extreme cold.

One of my favorite *Helleborus orientalis* hybrids, 'Old Early Purple', has dusky, dark-burgundy flowers visible in bud by Christmas and in bloom, usually, during January. A chance seedling of mine with pale-yellow flowers always opens a few wide-petaled blossoms just after the new year. On the wooded hillside, a dark, black-burgundy form from garden writer Elizabeth Lawrence's garden begins to bloom in January.

A few other perennials bloom along with the hellebores in my garden during winter's cold. Phloxes bloom all season, seldom in profusion, but always with a few flowers. They like winter sun and demand good drainage. The earliest of them to bloom, *Phlox nivalis* 'Camla', opens its large, bright-pink flowers above needlelike foliage as early as November. About a month later, *P. douglasii* 'Boothman's Variety', opens its purple-eyed, violet flowers. *P. subulata* from North Hills, the Vermont garden of Joe Eck and Wayne Winterrowd, blooms nearly all year with near-white flowers bearing crimson centers.

I'm fond of a number of winter-blooming irises as well. The Algerian iris (*Iris unguicularis*) first flowers about Thanksgiving. Slender, green leaf blades often hide the gray or beige buds that open to reveal fragrant, blue-purple flowers. This iris is dormant during the summer months and wants lime and a site in sun or part shade. Don't give it any additional watering during summer dry spells. *Iris reticulata* sends up its blue-gray leaves before the New Year, but the flowers wait until early February to open. It grows happily

I grow every species of hellebore except one, so I also have some that bloom later in the season. Depending on the species and variety, hellebore blooms begin in November and continue into April. Many self-sow, so I now have thousands naturalized in the shade of my woods. Other green-flowered hellebores that bloom in winter are *H. viridis, H. odorus, H. cyclophyllus, H. foetidus,* and *H. multifidus.*

The best-known hellebore, the Christmas rose (*H. niger*), blooms for me in late November. Because I have grown many seedlings from many different sources, I have some forms of *H. niger* that wait until March to bloom. Flowers vary in size and shape.

in ordinary soil—even if it's dry in summer—but blooms best with winter sun. Having collected a number of different cultivars, I now have blooms in many colors from early February until early April. Dark, burgundy-red 'Pauline' and 'Hercules' open first, the broader-petaled 'George' opens next, and the exquisite, near-white 'Natascha' is latest of all.

LITTLE BULBS BRIGHTEN THE LANDSCAPE

My first winter snowdrop, *Galanthus caucasicus*, appears in late November. This snowdrop blooms until *G. nivalis* begins just after Christmas. Both like winter sun and soil that is dry in summer and moist in winter. *G. elwesii* blooms a little later and by February, we find it throughout the woods and rock garden. This species is easy to identify by the green markings at the top and bottom of its down-turned cup. Some of the cups are entirely green. Before these species finish flowering, *G. ikariae* comes into bloom with broad, bright-green leaves and cups marked with green at the tips.

Along with the snowdrops, crocuses brighten the winter months. My winter-flowering crocuses, *Crocus imperati* ssp. *suaveolens* and *C. laevigatus*, usually appear by Christmas. *C. laevigatus* has fragrant, violet flowers feathered with purple on the outer petals, and *C. imperati* ssp. *suaveolens* has fragrant, violet flowers opening from creamy beige buds striped with purple. Another subspecies, *C. i.* ssp. *imperati*, has large but unscented flowers in January and February. Before they finish, *C. sieberi* begins blooming with white or violet flowers with yellow throats. In late February or early March, *C. s.* ssp. *sublimis* f. *tricolor* blooms with flowers having horizontal bands of violet, white, and yellow. Next come the tommies (*C. tommasinianus*) that

bloom in sun or shade with white, purple, or violet flowers. They look delicate but take the cold. By February, a flood of crocuses fills the rock garden, with *C. angustifolius*, *C. biflorus*, *C. olivieri*, *C. corsicus*, *C. minimus*, *C. vernus*, and others opening every day. Some of these species cross and self-sow, so every year there are new hybrids and seedlings to enjoy.

Crocuses grow as well beneath the shade of trees as they do in full sun. Winter sun produces better foliage that, in turn, produces corms that bloom the next year. Rodents find the corms delicious, but working a few stones into the soil when planting will help protect the plants.

Few genera match *Cyclamen* for year-round bloom. At Montrose, I can always find flowers on one or more species. The winter-flowering ones give me great pleasure, with variable leaves and small, sometimes fragrant flowers that show up against the bare, brown earth. Though they look fragile, I find perfect blooms even after nights when the temperature has dipped to 4°F. The first winter-

Crocus angustifolius adds a bright splash of color at ground level by February.

A Parade of Flowers from Fall to Spring

This chart shows the sequence, duration, and timing of blooms for the winter-flowering plants in Nancy Goodwin's North Carolina garden. These dates reflect the temperatures of a mild winter. A warmer or colder season, or a garden in a warmer or cooler USDA Hardiness Zone, could make the blooms earlier or later. Hardiness Zones are indicated in parentheses; (4) would indicate a plant hardy to Zone 4.

	Late November	Early December	Mid-December	Late December	Early January	Mid-January	Late January	Early February	Mid-February	Late February
HELLEBORES										
Helleborus vesicarius (6)					•	•	•	•	•	•
H. viridis (6)								•	•	•
H. odorus (6), *H. cyclophyllus* (6), *H. multifidus* (7)									•	•
H. orientalis hybrids (6), *H. niger* (3), *H. n.* ssp. *macranthus* (4)	•	•	•	•	•	•	•	•	•	•
PHLOX										
Phlox nivalis 'Camla' (6), *P. subulata* (from North Hills) (3)	•	•	•	•	•	•	•	•	•	•
P. douglasii 'Boothman's Variety' (5)			•	•	•	•	•	•	•	•
IRIS										
Iris unguicularis (7)	•	•	•	•	•	•	•	•	•	•
Iris reticulata (5)								•	•	•
SNOWDROPS										
Galanthus caucasicus (5)	•	•	•	•	•	•	•	•	•	•
G. nivalis (4)			•	•	•	•	•	•	•	•
G. elwesii (4)						•	•	•	•	•
G. ikariae (4)								•	•	•
CROCUS										
Crocus laevigatus (5)	•	•	•	•	•					
C. imperati ssp. *suaveolens* (5)	•	•	•	•			•			
C. i. ssp. *imperati* (5)						•	•	•	•	
C. sieberi (3)					•	•	•	•	•	•
C. olivieri (5), *C. s.* ssp. *sublimis* f. *tricolor* (3)						•	•	•	•	
C. tommasinianus (3)						•	•	•	•	•
C. corsicus (7), *C. biflorus* (3)							•	•	•	•
C. vernus (4), *C. minimus* (3)							•	•	•	•
C. angustifolius (3)						•	•	•	•	
CYCLAMEN										
Cyclamen coum (5)	•	•	•	•	•	•	•	•	•	•
C. trochopteranthum (7)								•	•	•
C. pseudibericum (8)				•	•	•	•	•	•	
WOODY PLANTS										
Jasminum nudiflorum (6), *Clematis cirrhosa* (7)	•	•	•	•	•	•	•	•	•	•
Lonicera fragrantissima (5), *Hamamelis* × *intermedia* (5), *Prunus mume* (6)					•	•	•	•	•	•

flowering cyclamen to bloom here at Montrose, *Cyclamen coum*, appears beneath the bare branches of our dawn redwood (*Metasequoia glyptostroboides*) about Thanksgiving. This early flowering Russian form has heart-shaped leaves beautifully marked with silver, and flowers that are white, pink, or dark crimson. Shortly after Christmas, more *C. coum* bloom beneath our Himalayan cedar (*Cedrus deodara*) and in the woods. By the end of January, they are everywhere. In February, *C. trochopteranthum* opens its distinctive, twisted petals. Last year, I had a few *C. pseudibericum* flowers by Christmas and masses by February. This species has large, pink to dark red-violet flowers with black at the mouth above a margin of white.

FLOWERING SHRUBS ADD TO WINTER'S SHOW

Some woody plants and vines brighten the landscape with flowers and fragrance. By Thanksgiving, we see bright yellow buds with touches of red on winter yellow jasmine (*Jasminum nudiflorum*) planted in full sun. The slightly peachy fragrance of winter honeysuckle (*Lonicera fragrantissima*) tempts us to breathe deeply the aroma of its creamy white, pink-tinged flowers, which open along bare, silver-gray stems. The earliest winter-flowering witch hazel (*Hamamelis* × *intermedia*) at Montrose is 'James Wells', which is a bright-yellow-flowered shrub that's usually in bloom by mid-January. A little later, 'Jelena' opens with golden yellow and coral petals that look like twisted threads.

Witch hazels aren't fussy about soil. They bloom well in high shade in our somewhat acid, clay loam. Fragrant Japanese apricots (*Prunus mume*) begin to bloom whenever we have a mild spell. They like full sun but will also flower in part shade where the shelter of

"Some woody plants and vines brighten the landscape with flowers and fragrance."

overhanging branches may protect blossoms from untimely freezes. The cultivar 'Peggy Clarke' often opens its single pink flowers as early as January, while the dark, crimson-flowered 'Kobai' waits until later.

Clematis cirrhosa produces bright green leaves as it recovers from summer's heat. Pendant, creamy yellow, fragrant flowers appear in the rafters of our lath house, growing so high we have to stand at a distance to see them. It bears fluffy seed clusters that look like puffs of snow among the flowers.

By the end of February, the swollen flower buds on the elms become racemes of brownish-green flowers, and the maples show their red clusters of stamens. Owls call to each other at twilight. We know it is spring.

Helleborus foetidus bears distinctive evergreen foliage and greenish flowers.

STEVE SCHMIDT

is owner of American Ornamental Perennials, a wholesale nursery specializing in ornamental grasses and perennials. He has served as a regional director for the Perennial Plant Association.

Grasses *Waken the* Winter Garden

(FAR LEFT) Masses of grasses make a strong visual statement. Here, the tall *Miscanthus floridulus*, fountain grass, and purple moor grass (*Molinia caerulea*) create a rich, airy tapestry above a cluster of *Sedum* 'Autumn Joy'.

(INSET) At 12 ft. high, ravenna grass makes a dramatic display. Even with several feet of snow, its slender seed heads stand tall.

M Y PARENTS ALWAYS had the most colorful yard in the neighborhood. All spring and summer it was ablaze with the blooms of perennials, azaleas, roses, peonies, and daylilies. As a child, I liked to toddle along at their side while they tended the gardens and introduced me to the bright colors of pansies, the delicate fragrance of lily of the valley, and the glorious flowers of the peonies. Those were lessons I never forgot. But when I grew up and moved across the country to Eagle Creek, Oregon, I learned a whole new set of garden lessons, and they had nothing at all to do with bold colors, sweet scents, or flowery blossoms. In fact, they had little to do even with summer. Out west, you see, I fell for a weed.

At least that's what ornamental grasses were to most folks a decade ago; nobody thought of them as proper garden plants. But grasses caught my eye right away. I liked their bold textures, many shades of colors, and luminous

153

variegation. I liked their swaying motions when the wind blew, and the soft, rustling sounds they made. They seemed so unusual and so beautiful. I fell in love with them.

GRASSES GIVE LIFE TO THE GARDEN IN FALL AND WINTER

Outside my kitchen window, the January sky is steel gray; the nip in the air suggests snow. Even though my perennials have been reduced to spindly, broken stalks and mushy, disintegrating mounds, it's still exciting to look out at the stately skeletons of my ornamental grasses as they dance in the wind and wave their airy seed heads proud as flags. Their tawny colors add a golden glow of warmth to the season's monotonous monochromes. It took me a few years to realize it, but their striking fall and winter presence was all the more reason to use grasses in the garden.

Grasses also give life to the winter garden by creating a natural environment that brings wildlife into my yard. The food, shelter, and windbreak they provide attract birds and small animals. Sometimes I see wrens and chickadees perched in the feathery grass flowers, dining safely on seeds in the shelter of grassy foliage. Rabbits aren't always welcome in my perennial border, but they, too, find food and shelter in the clumps of grasses. Many other animals, including predators like coyotes and foxes, slink through the thickets of my grass garden.

Grasses are remarkably adaptable garden plants. There are perennial and annual varieties, but it's the perennials that stand up to winter; annuals usually wilt away at the end of the season. Perennial grasses look good almost anywhere, particularly when planted en masse. Singly or in groups, they add surprising

visual impact to island beds and borders and can work wonders as screens for unsightly sheds and fences, or as a soft, billowy counterpoint to a tall building.

Grasses also look great when several varieties are mixed together. To my eye, blue oat grass (*Helictotrichon sempervirens*) and leatherleaf sedge (*Carex buchananii*) make an especially striking pair.

No matter where or how they are planted, grasses are always changing, reflecting the passage of seasons. When the weather cools, the color slowly drains from warm-season grasses, leaving them with light-brown foliage. A few genus like *Miscanthus*, *Panicum*, and *Erianthus* retain a touch of color in fall, with red- or orange-tinged foliage.

Cool-season grasses, such as leatherleaf sedge and blue oat grass, stay mostly evergreen in winter. Their presence brings color to the winter garden with foliage in shades of blue, bronze-brown, and green.

(ABOVE) Combine grasses for a striking effect. Maiden grass and the slightly smaller fountain grass are two that can be used to create a strong composition.

(LEFT) Evergreen grasses provide year-round good looks. This blue oat grass shines in spring when the pink bloom of hyacinths provide a colorful counterpoint.

Switch grass brightens the late-season garden with a colorful wave of seed heads. Here, they crash over a planting of lavender and *Sedum* 'Autumn Joy'.

LARGER GRASSES CREATE A PRESENCE IN THE LANDSCAPE

The larger perennial grasses like some *Miscanthus* species, ravenna grass (*Erianthus ravennae*), and others that grow to 4 ft. tall or more are best for creating hedges, screens, or dramatic mass plantings. They also work well as specimen plants in beds or borders.

And of all the larger grasses, I think *Miscanthus* is the most versatile genus. These grasses range from the stately 8-ft. to 12-ft. towers of giant *Miscanthus floridulus* to the elegant, vase-shaped stands of 5-ft.- to 6-ft.-tall

"For a colorful, all-season ornamental grass, it's hard to beat blue oat grass."

maiden grass (*M. sinensis* 'Gracillimus'), and the diminutive, yet graceful, 3-ft.- to 4-ft.-high *M. sinensis* 'Yaku Jima'. They put punch in my garden from July to mid-February.

'Gracillimus' is a real standout. Its graceful arches never fail to captivate my eye, and the plant is a jack-of-all-trades in the garden. I've used it to create bold, undulating backgrounds, to screen an unsightly shed, as a specimen, in groups both large and small, and to accent water features. Some gardeners prize 'Gracillimus' for its cut flowers, which look like a cluster of outstretched fingers at the end of a long, narrow stem. The fountaining foliage of *Miscanthus* helps propel the garden through the winter months. Some *Miscanthus* species, such as *M. floridulus*, thrive in USDA Hardiness Zone 4, and flourish throughout the continental United States and much of Canada. Most cultivars are more tender, so check the hardiness range of any *Miscanthus* before making a purchase.

Ravenna grass (*Saccharum ravennae*, formerly known as *Erianthus ravennae*) is one of the most striking of all ornamental grasses. Its sheer size—ravenna grass reaches heights of up to 9 ft. to 12 ft.—gives it a dramatic presence. It flowers in late summer with towering, broad, silvery white inflorescences shining against wine-purple flower stems. The foliage, green-gray in summer, picks up tints of purple and orange in the fall, then turns buff-brown in the winter. Snow makes this grass even more attractive, by putting a cloak of sparkling white over its foliage. Ravenna grass thrives in Zones 6 to 9 (−10°F to 20°F).

SMALLER GRASSES SHINE IN BORDERS AND BEDS

Smaller grasses, those that top out at 4 ft. or less, also make dramatic mass plantings, but I think they look best when integrated with other perennials in beds and borders. One of the grasses best suited for an understated role in the garden is actually a sedge, the leatherleaf sedge (*Carex buchananii*). It looks much like a grass, but differs by virtue of its different flowers and its solid, usually triangular stems. I think of leatherleaf sedge as a blender-and-weaver plant. The 1-ft.- to 2-ft.-tall tufts of reddish-bronze foliage aren't much by themselves but when combined with plants with blue or red foliage and flowers, the contrast makes them seem brighter. In winter, this sedge maintains its robust, bronzy hue, adding interest and color to landscapes of snow and evergreens. Leatherleaf sedge is hardy in Zones 7 to 9 and thrives in well-drained, amended soil.

For a colorful, all-season ornamental grass, it's hard to beat blue oat grass. I consider it a real gem; it always looks good and can be used in a variety of situations. It is stunning as a single specimen and in groupings, and it mixes well with almost any perennial or shrub, particularly when paired with leatherleaf sedge. The blue foliage is always a standout in the winter garden, lending a spot of color to otherwise barren landscapes. Blue oat grass, also known as blue avena grass, grows 2 ft. to 3 ft. high. In my garden it flowers profusely in late May, with golden inflorescences reaching 4 ft. to 6 ft. high. Blue oat grass is hardy in Zones 4 to 8, grows well in most soils, and prefers full sun. It will stand light shade, but struggles to survive in deep shade.

Fountain grass (*Pennisetum alopecuroides*) stars in the summer garden, but carries well into autumn and winter. With a soft, mounding form and muted color, fountain grass is most effective in masses. It only grows 2 ft. to 4 ft. high, mixing well with black-eyed Susan (*Rudbeckia fulgida* var. *sullivantii* 'Goldsturm') or *Sedum* 'Autumn Joy', to create classic plant combinations with long-season interest.

Fountain grass is crowned with purplish-pink seed heads that are striking in summer but gradually turn buff-colored in autumn and then begin to disintegrate in winter. The rich, green foliage fades too, gradually turning beige-brown. In late winter, before new growth starts, it should be cut back to 4 in. to 6 in. Fountain grass thrives in Zones 5 to 9.

Another good garden-scale grass is switch grass (*Panicum virgatum*), a member of the genus that once stood tall in the prairies of the American Midwest. Gardeners like this handsome North American native for its decorative

Create colorful contrasts by combining leatherleaf sedge and plants with red or blue foliage or flowers. The fall colors of dwarf plumbago (*Cerato-stigma plumbaginades*) look brighter next to the sedge's bronzy fronds.

quality, but it was once appreciated more as feed for livestock and wildlife. Like so many of our native plants, switch grass was adopted by European hybridizers who reintroduced improved varieties to the U.S. The Germans created one of the best cultivars, *Panicum virgatum* 'Rehbraun'. It reaches up to 3 ft. tall in my garden, takes on a fiery glow in autumn, and then fades to reddish brown in winter. It stands up to wind better than most plants; its delicate seed heads are rarely ravaged by even the strongest gusts. A dusting of light snow drapes an enchanting mantle on switch grass' shoulders. Even if heavy snowfall knocks it to the ground, this switch grass usually bounces back and seldom looks worse for the wear. Another favorite cultivar is the slightly taller 'Heavy Metal'. Its steel-blue foliage rises 3 ft. or 4 ft. in height and in summer is crowned by a delicate-looking mist of pink flowers. Switch grasses are hardy in Zones 4 to 9.

TREAT GRASSES LIKE OTHER PERENNIALS

Ornamental grass gardening is fun and easy. Most grasses require the same conditions as other herbaceous perennials, so you won't go wrong planting them in well-drained, friable soil amended with plenty of compost.

Most grasses perform best in full sun, but there's no need to worry if you've got shade. They also grow in less than ideal conditions, though they might not get quite as tall, and they may need staking to help keep them upright.

Grasses are best planted in spring, when new growth begins, but they can be planted anytime the ground can be worked. Grasses are

Fountain grass flaunts its feathery plumes, creating a striking display in the late summer garden.

usually purchased in containers, and once out of the pot, you may discover that the plant's roots are congested and coiling around the soil. If so, use a knife to score the roots, then tease them out. If you've purchased the grasses from a mail-order source, they may arrive bare-root. If so, remove them from the box as soon as possible and check for desiccation. If the plants look dried out, put them into a pail of water in a shady spot for an hour or so while you prepare a planting hole, and amend the hole with compost or other organic material.

The least understood aspect of planting grasses is giving them proper spacing. It's easy for plantings to become too crowded after a few growing seasons. A simple rule of thumb is to plant grasses as far apart as their height. If a grass grows 3 ft. tall, plant it 3 ft. from its neighbor. But if you're mixing varieties, the rule changes a little. Plant mixed pairs as far apart as the height of the taller plant. If you're planting a grass that gets 4 ft. tall next to one that grows only 1 ft. high, you'll need to plant them 4 ft. apart. The plantings might look sparse at first, but grasses fill out quickly. If you need a lot of plants to fill out a large area, you can divide clumps into quarters every other year or so. Divisions are best made in early spring.

When you put the grass in the ground, add a little fertilizer. I prefer a slow-release type that will feed the plant throughout the season; a fertilizer with an 18-6-12 NPK ratio would be ideal. After their first year, most grasses do not need fertilizer.

After planting a grass, be sure to water it deeply. Grasses need regular, deep watering during their first season, but should be allowed to dry out between drinks. Once established, they are drought-tolerant.

Finish your planting by adding 4 in. or 5 in. of mulch. It will help protect the grass' roots

"A simple rule of thumb is to plant grasses as far apart as their height."

and stems from winter cold and summer heat. Mulch helps keep the soil from drying out too.

Most ornamental grasses require cutting back only once a year, in late winter. You can use a hand pruner, but if you've got a lot of grasses, try a power weed or hedge trimmer. Timing may depend on your personal preferences, but the important thing is to cut grasses back to 4 in. to 6 in. aboveground before new growth begins. Grasses that stay mostly evergreen should be cleaned up with a rake and trimmed of any dead foliage in early spring. Remember, if a grass dies back, cut it back. I actually like cutting the grasses. This annual ritual is a reminder that the soil will soon be warming and that another season of growth will soon be under way. Even in winter, grasses remind me of the spring to come.

Maiden grass stands tall in the winter snow, remaining a handsome garden specimen throughout the winter.

SYDNEY EDDISON

teaches gardening at the New York Botanical Garden. The author of four gardening books, including *The Self-Taught Gardener*, she writes for several publications and lectures widely.

Autumn's *Blazing* Beauties

Enkianthus earns a starring role in late-fall productions, as its fine color deftly illuminates many a November landscape.

ALL GARDENERS REJOICE when winter teeters on the brink of spring. Most welcome the first warm days of summer, and after enduring the dog days of August, rush to embrace the fall. But not many anticipate the passage of fall into winter with the same enthusiasm. I find myself in that minority, as I love this particular period of transition.

November skies can be wonderful. As the leaves fall to the ground, views through the forest that surrounds our garden suddenly open up. For the first time in six months we can see the sun rise and set, and the sky seems to expand. Individual beams of sunlight pierce the clouds like spotlights. Caught in their glancing rays, the lingering golden foliage of Chinese witch hazel takes my breath away. And this is not the only shrub in our garden that comes into its own at this time of year.

Even after its leaves drop, the flowers of common witch hazel remain to greet the coming of winter with vibrant color.

Witch hazel and fothergilla, two members of the family Hamamelidaceae, greet the verge of winter with a brilliant show of color. In my garden, these two, along with redvein enkianthus, Virginia sweetspire, and oakleaf hydrangea, make November a month worth waiting for instead of a prelude to discontent. On a smaller scale, they rekindle and prolong the fading fall colors of the surrounding forest. Although the native habitats of these shrubs are at the edges of shady woodlands, all of mine tolerate and indeed flower just fine in full to part sun.

ENKIANTHUS PROVIDES A MIX OF ORANGE, RED, AND YELLOW

If redvein enkianthus (*Enkianthus campanulatus*) had a catchy common name, it would be in every garden. Beautiful and easy to grow, its

neat habit and fairly small size make it useful as a centerpiece in a small, suburban garden or as part of a shrub planting in a larger, country garden. In mid- to late October, the foliage turns the most amazing shades of orange and red, with a few purple leaves as well.

By a stroke of good luck, I planted a witch hazel on an east-facing slope in front of, but below, a mature redvein enkianthus. In this accidental pairing, the hot, fall colors of the enkianthus leaves provide a vivid background for the cool, yellow haze of the witch hazel blossoms each fall.

Fabulous color is not this shrub's only charm. Enkianthus leaves gather in tufts at the ends of twigs, with pronounced intervals between each twig. The tiers of foliage are reminiscent of native dogwood (*Cornus florida*), but the linear pattern of its branches is quite different. As dogwood branches reach out horizontally, those of the enkianthus angle upward, close to the main trunk. This gives it a narrower silhouette. In addition to this interesting growth habit, the bark is as tight, gray, and sensuously smooth as the bark of a beech tree.

Spring brings clusters of flowers that resemble lily-of-the-valley bells to the terminal buds of every twig. The flowers on my shrub are cream-colored, veined, and edged with pink. There is also a red-flowering form reputed to be very showy. Truly a plant for all seasons, fall is still the finest hour for this superb shrub.

WITCH HAZELS' GOLDEN HUES STEAL THE FALL SHOW

For shades of yellow and gold, there is no shrub to beat witch hazels in autumn. Chinese witch hazel (Hamamelis mollis) was one of the first shrubs I planted in my garden, and it remains first in my affections, though I do profess a weakness for any witch hazel. Its leaves are soft to the touch, and in mid- to late October they turn a magnificent gold color that lasts for three to six weeks or more. After the color fades, the leaves turn brown, curl in upon themselves, and hang from the twigs like fragile cocoons, waiting for wispy, yellow flowers to appear among them in February or March.

Although the *H. mollis* is my favorite for its spectacular fall color and fragrant spring flowers, the native common witch hazel (*H. virginiana*) is also dear to my heart. Common witch hazel is an understory plant that can become leggy if it has to struggle for the light. But in the open, it develops into a graceful, spreading shrub about 20 ft. tall.

The broad leaves of common witch hazel are similar to those of *H. mollis*, but turn a

Chinese witch hazel is worth its weight in gold, as its honey-colored foliage serves as a beacon in late fall landscapes.

Common witch hazel does double duty in fall. Pale yellow foliage shares the spotlight with diminutive yellow blossoms.

clear, bright yellow instead of gold. The abundance of pale yellow fall flowers that accompany the colored foliage comes as a wonderful, late-season surprise. The deceptively fragile-looking blossoms that appear near the end of October keep winter at bay for weeks.

Shrubs to Carry the Garden from Fall into Winter   by Michael Dirr

Not only do these shrubs offer dazzling fall color but frosts and freezes intensify their brilliance. Expect a long-lasting show as these leaves will hang on when all other leaves have fallen. All of these shrubs grow well sited in full sun to part shade and in well-drained soil, unless otherwise noted. The larger shrubs can be pruned to limit their size in the home landscape.

NAME	FALL COLOR CHARACTERISTICS	HEIGHT	CULTURAL CONDITIONS	HARDINESS ZONES
Berberis koreana (Korean barberry)	red	4 to 6 ft.	Very tolerant shrub	3 to 7
Berberis × mentorensis (mentor barberry)	red	5 to 7 ft.	Very tolerant shrub	5 to 8
Berberis thunbergii (Japanese barberry)	red	3 to 6 ft.	Full sun for best color	4 to 8
Calycanthus floridus (sweetshrub)	yellow	6 to 10 ft.	Performs well in good light	5 to 9
Clethra alnifolia (summersweet)	yellow	3 to 8 ft.	Likes acid, moist soil	4 to 9
Cornus alba (tatarian dogwood)	red	8 to 10 ft.	Very tolerant shrub	2 to 6
Enkianthus campanulatus (redvein enkianthus)	yellow, orange, red	6 to 15 ft.	Likes acid, moist soil	4 to 7
Fothergilla gardenii (dwarf fothergilla)	yellow, orange, red	2 to 3 ft.	Likes acid soil	5 to 9
Fothergilla major (large fothergilla)	yellow, orange, red	6 to 10 ft.	Likes acid soil	4 to 8
Hamamelis × intermedia (hybrid witch hazel)	yellow, orange, red	10 to 20 ft.	Likes organic, moist soil	5 to 8
Hamamelis japonica (Japanese witch hazel)	yellow, orange, red	10 to 15 ft.	Likes organic, moist soil	5 to 8
Hamamelis mollis (Chinese witch hazel)	yellow and orange	10 to 15 ft.	Likes organic, moist soil	5 to 8
Hamamelis vernalis (vernal witch hazel)	yellow	6 to 10 ft.	Likes organic, moist soil	4 to 8
Hamamelis virginiana (common witch hazel)	yellow	15 to 20 ft.	Likes organic, moist soil	3 to 8
Hydrangea quercifolia (oakleaf hydrangea)	red	4 to 6 ft.	Likes acid soil	5 to 9
Itea virginica (Virginia sweetspire)	yellow, orange, red	3 to 5 ft.	Very tolerant shrub	5 to 9
Spiraea × bumalda (Bumald spirea cultivars)	yellow and red	3 to 4 ft.	Prefers full sun	4 to 8
Spiraea japonica (Japanese spirea cultivars)	yellow and red	4 to 5 ft.	Very tolerant shrub	4 to 8
Spiraea prunifolia (bridalwreath spirea)	orange and red	4 to 9 ft.	Very tolerant shrub	4 to 8
Spiraea thunbergii (Thunberg spirea)	yellow and orange	3 to 5 ft.	Very tolerant shrub	4 to 8
Vaccinium angustifolium (lowbush blueberry)	red	½ to 2 ft.	Likes acid soil	2 to 5
Vaccinium corymbosum (highbush blueberry)	yellow and red	6 to 12 ft.	Likes acid soil	3 to 7
Viburnum dilatatum (linden viburnum)	red	8 to 10 ft.	Very tolerant shrub	5 to 7
Viburnum prunifolium (blackhaw viburnum)	red	12 to 15 ft.	Does well in dry soils	3 to 9
Viburnum rufidulum (rusty blackhaw viburnum)	red	10 to 20 ft.	Very tolerant shrub	5 to 9
Xanthorhiza simplicissima (yellowroot)	yellow and orange	2 to 3 ft.	Very tolerant shrub	3 to 9
Zenobia pulverulenta (dusty zenobia)	yellow	2 to 3 ft.	Likes acid, moist soil	5 to 9

Michael Dirr is the author of Dirr's Hardy Trees and Shrubs *and the* Manual of Woody Landscape Plants.

FOTHERGILLA MAKES A BONFIRE LOOK DULL

The flamboyant red, orange, and purple autumn display of my enkianthus mirrors my *Fothergilla gardenii*—a much smaller native plant. Like enkianthus, fothergilla has no common name, though the botanical name is no more difficult than *Forsythia*. In 1990, this dainty, 3-ft. to 4-ft. shrub was among a handful to win the Pennsylvania Horticultural Society's Gold Medal Award. The award, given nearly every year since 1978, promotes beauti-

ful, hardy, easy-to-grow plants that deserve wider use.

An eminently deserving plant, fothergilla boasts fuzzy, white flowers in the spring, summer foliage that resembles a witch hazel's, and fall colors that make a bonfire look dull in comparison. Because of its small stature, this plant cries out for company. It can be used effectively in a perennial border, or even among evergreens in a foundation planting. The dark green leaves of rhododendrons are perfect to set off its autumn brilliance.

Fothergilla sustains fall's brilliance by showcasing its vibrant red, yellow, and orange leaves through November.

Plant oakleaf hydrangea if only for its lush color. Nothing rivals the richness of its deep burgundy-red leaves in late autumn.

BURGUNDY REDS OF HYDRANGEA AND SWEETSPIRE INTENSIFY IN FALL

Moroccan red leather is the best description for the autumn foliage color of both oakleaf hydrangea (*Hydrangea quercifolia*) and Virginia sweetspire (*Itea virginica* 'Henry's Garnet'), two more native shrubs that both hold onto their leaves well into December in my garden.

The oakleaf hydrangea is a large, rangy shrub that grows 6 ft. to 8 ft. high and about the same across. Its lobed, pebbly textured, dark green leaves are very handsome throughout the summer. But, in the fall, the green foliage gives way to a rich, dark burgundy color that gives this shrub the masculine appeal of

the leather upholstery one might find in an old-fashioned British club. In a large perennial border, the oakleaf hydrangea makes a fine structural plant, and it is also beautiful planted at the edge of woodlands.

Virginia sweetspire has a more refined growth habit, developing into a thicket of slender, arching branches clad in narrow, pointed leaves. As the stems around the outside of the clump are shorter than those in the center, its form is rounded. My original plant, now six years old and about 4 ft. tall, started out in a perennial bed, but its habit of layering and producing suckers made me fear for neighboring herbaceous plants. It now forms a distinct, 6-ft.-wide mound at the end of a shrub border. The tendency of Virginia sweetspire to wander limits its use in perennial borders, but makes it a natural choice for steep banks or at the edge of a pond.

By mid- to late October, the foliage of sweetspire almost matches that of the hydrangea in color. But its leaves are shiny instead of rough textured, and appear to be a lighter, brighter red touched here and there with crimson. The stems, which become visible through the thinning leaves, are also red tinted. At Thanksgiving, cut branches of sweetspire make a colorful addition to my indoor bouquets of hardy chrysanthemums.

While autumn is the climax of their garden performances, both sweetspires and oakleaf hydrangeas have worthwhile flowers. Here, hydrangeas bloom in July and have large, conical heads of massed, sterile flowers—white at first, but turning a soft green with a touch of pink as the season progresses. The sweetspires bloom in June, producing lax, 6-in.-long spires of tiny, white flowers.

RICH FOLIAGE BOOSTS OFF-SEASON INTEREST

Lucky is the gardener who falls in love with foliage first and flowers second, but that is not the nature of the beast. Only when disappointment in the fleeting beauty of perennials drives gardeners to the shrub section of the nursery do they realize the value of leaves, growth habit, and off-season appeal.

In the beginning, I was seduced by spring and summer flowers. Then it was herbaceous foliage plants, and finally, evergreens and deciduous shrubs. Now, after a lifetime of gardening, I value most those plants that provide something to look at in all four seasons. And I have a particular admiration for the deciduous shrubs that do not go gently into the dark night of winter, but flare up like beacons in the autumn landscape.

Crimson-colored sweetspire continues to provide garden interest even after all other trees have lost their leaves.

Credits

PHOTOS

Front matter

Jodie Delohery, © The Taunton Press, Inc.—p. ii
Steve Silk, © The Taunton Press, Inc.—p. iii
Virginia Small, © The Taunton Press, Inc.; Steve Silk, © The Taunton Press, Inc.; © David Cavagnaro, © Susan Roth (top), Steve Silk, © The Taunton Press, Inc. (bottom)—Contents (from left)
Steve Silk, © The Taunton Press, Inc.—p. 2

Part I: Design Techniques

Jodie Delohery, © The Taunton Press, Inc.—pp. 4, 6, 7 (New York Botanical Garden), 9 (bottom, New York Botanical Garden), 17
Lee Anne White, © The Taunton Press, Inc.—pp. 5, 8 (New York Botanical Garden), 10 (top, Wesley Rouse garden), 13 (Bellevue Botanic Garden)
Steve Silk, © The Taunton Press, Inc.—pp. 9 (top, Wesley Rouse garden, Southbury, Conn.), 11 (Bellevue Botanic Garden, Bellevue, Wash.), 20, 22–26, 28–31
© Douglas Ruhren—p. 12 (Montrose, Hillsborough, N.C.)
Virginia Small, © The Taunton Press, Inc.—pp. 14, 16, 18, 19

Part II: Working with Color

© Clive Nichols—pp. 34, 39 (courtesy *Planting Companions;* Stewart, Tabori & Chang), 82 (Savill Gardens, Berkshire)
Chris Curless, © The Taunton Press, Inc.—p. 36
© Dency Kane—pp. 40, 42, 43 (bottom), 45, 47
Susan Kahn—p. 43 (top)
Mark Kane, © The Taunton Press, Inc.—p. 44
© David Cavagnaro—pp. 46, 78–79
Steve Silk, © The Taunton Press, Inc.—pp. 32, 48, 50–55
Delilah Smittle, © The Taunton Press, Inc.—pp. 56, 60, 61
© Keeyla Meadows—pp. 33, 58

Part III: Special Plantings

Lee Anne White, © The Taunton Press, Inc.—pp. 64, 66–68, 70, 72–75, 98
Bard Wrigley—p. 65 (author photo)
© Allan Mandell—pp. 62, 78 (left), 94, 97, 103–105
Steve Silk, © The Taunton Press, Inc.—pp. 69, 84, 88, 91
© David Cavagnaro—p. 78 (right)
© Susan Roth—p. 80
© Charles Mann—p. 81

© Vincent Laurence—p. 92
© J. Paul Moore—pp. 63, 100, 102
Todd Meier, © The Taunton Press, Inc.—pp. 106, 106–107, 109–111, 113

Part IV: Year-Round Interest

© Carole Otteson—pp. 114, 116, 123 (bottom)
Virginia Small, © The Taunton Press, Inc.—pp. 117, 119 (all except bottom left), 122, 123 (top)
Lee Anne White, © The Taunton Press, Inc.—pp. 119 (bottom left), 120, 121, 146 (all except top right), 148–151
Bard Wrigley—p. 25 (author photo)
Delilah Smittle, © The Taunton Press, Inc.—pp. 124, 126 (top)
© Susan Roth—pp. 126 (bottom), 156, 158, 160, 160–161 (small photo)
© J. Paul Moore—pp. 127, 162, 165, 167
© Harrison Flint—p. 128 (top)
© Clive Nichols—pp. 128 (bottom), 129
Steve Silk, © The Taunton Press, Inc.—pp. 115, 130, 132, 133, 135–137, 141, 146 (top right), 152–153 (small photo)
Saxon Holt—p. 147
© Roger Foley—pp. 152, 155, 159
© Michael S. Thompson—pp. 154, 157
© Michael Dirr—p. 163
© Ken Druse—p. 166

ILLUSTRATIONS

Hans Hofmann, The Golden Wall, 1961, 151 x 182 cm, Mr. and Mrs. Frank G. Logan Prize Fund. Photograph © 1997, The Art Institute of Chicago. All Rights Reserved—p. 35
Georgia O'Keeffe, White Rose with Larkspur No. 2, Henry H. and Zoe Oliver Sherman Fund, courtesy Museum of Fine Arts, Boston—p. 37
Gary Williamson—p. 38
Keeyla Meadows—p. 59
Jeni Webber—p. 77
Vince Babak—pp. 86, 87
Sally Bensusen—p. 96
Michael Gellatly—pp. 108, 112
Richard James Cook—p. 134

Index

Note: Page references in bold indicate a drawing; page references in italics indicate a photograph.

Japanese maples, 29, *29*, 31, 142, *145*
Jasmine, 150, 151
Joe Pye weed, *8*
Junipers, *14*, *18*, 30, *30*, 133, 134, *134*, 135, 136

K

Kangaroo paw, 98
Kieffer pear trees, 109, 113
Knotweed, 98

L

Lady's mantle, 99
Lamb's ear, 39, 98, 99
Lavender, 98, 99
Leaf size contrasts, *6*, *8*, *10*, 11, *11*
Licorice plant, *46*
Lilacs, 99
Lilies, *45*, 46, 52, *58*, 61
Lilyturf, 61, 98, 99
Lobelia, 61
Loosestrife, 102
Louisiana iris, 103
Love-in-a-mist, *23*

M

Magnolias, 109
Maples, 29, *29*, 31, 142
Marigolds, 58
Mass plantings, 11–12, *12*, 13, *14*, 15–16, *16*
  accent color or texture, *16*, 19–20
  annuals as fillers, 19
  combining forms and textures, 17, *17*, 18
  drifts, *14*, 18, *18*
  of plants with seedpods/seedheads, *118*, 121–22
  proportion of, 17, *17*, 18
  role/relation to other garden elements, 16, *16*
Masterwort, 105
Meadowsweet, *104*, 105
Milkweed, 119
Mints, *97*
Mock orange, 128, *129*
Money plant, 118, 120, *123*
Mountain clethra, 142
Mullien, *22*

O

Oregano, 99

P

Pasque flower, *135*, 136
Paths/pathways, *92*, 93–94
  curving and meandering, 95
  path materials, *92*, 94, *94*, **96**, *97*, 98
  planted, *92*, 93, 95
  plants for paths, *92*, 94, 97, *97*, 98, *98*, 99
Pear tree cultivars, 109
Peonies, 102
Perspective, forcing, 87, **87**, 88, 90–91
Phlox, 9, 99, 148, 150
Pines, 28, *28*, 55, 132, 142, 144
Pinks, 58, 98, 99
Plant forms and shapes, *9*, *11*, 13, *13*
Pocketbook flower, 61
Pollarding, 26, *26*
Poppies, *24*, 120, *120*
Porcupine grass, *116*

Prairie mallows, 104
Pruning:
  as an art, 28–29
  for espaliers, *109*, 111–12, **112**, 113, *113*
  snapping "candles," 28, *28*
Pussytoes, *24*

R

Redhot poker, 99
Repetition, 8–9, *9*
Rhododendrons, 141, 165
Rice paper plant, 11
River birches, *139*, 142
Rose of Sharon, 109
Roses, 58, 99
Russian hawthorn, *23*
Russian pincushion, *23*

S

Sages, *16*, 58, 99
Salvias, 11, *42*, 46, 58, 61
Scented shrubs, *124*, 125–26
  choosing by scent, 129
  fragrant plants to consider, 127–29
  temperature and time of day, 126, 129
Sea holly, *11*
Sedges, 54, *55*, 99
Sedums, *14*, *97*, *116*, 121, 137, *145*
Seedpods/seedheads, *116*, 117, 119
  appearance and function of, 119, *119*
  for arrangements, 121–22
  combining textures of, 22, *23*, 24
  with light-catching grasses, 122, *122*, 123
  mass plantings of, *118*, 121–22
  plants featuring, 118
  seasonal features of, 123, *123*
See-through plants, 13
Shiso, 45
Shrubs, 11
  autumn-to-winter varieties, 164
  pruning and sculpting, 28–29, 31
  scented, *124*, 125–29
  for winter gardens, 150, 151
Siberian iris, 13, 102–103, *103*
Smoke tree, *8*, 50, *52*, 55
Snakeroot, 55
Sneezeweed, 45
Snowdrops, 149, 150
Sorrel, 99
Speedwell, 104
Spiderwort, 105
Spireas, 55, 162, 164
Spruces, 132, 133, 134, 135
Spurges, 55, 61, 98, 99
Spurias, *103*, 103–104
Stone paths/pathways, *92*, 94, *94*, **96**, *97*, 98
Strawberry shrub, 127
Summersweet, *127*, 128, 162, 164
Sunflowers, 41, *44*, 46, 120
Sweet box, 127, *128*
Sweet pepperbush, 128
Sweet-potato vine, 45
Sweet shrub, 126, *126*, 127
Sweetspire, 164, 166, *167*
Sweet woodruff, 99

T

Textures, combining, *8*, 11, *11*, *20*, 21, *22*
  hardscape materials for, *22*, 23–24, *24*, 25, *25*
  restraint and balancing of, *22*, 25

seasonal features of plants, *22*, *23*, 24
seedhead/seedpod features, *22*, *23*, 24
size differences, *22*, *23*–24, *24*
Thorny elaeagnus, *128*, 129
Thyme, *97*, 99, 136
Tickseed, 121–22
Trees, 109, 113
Trees, pruning and sculpting, 26, *26*, 27
  for an allée, *84*, 86–87
  bonsai features, 26, *26*, 29, *29*
  cloud-like foliage technique, 28, *28*
  encouraging new growth, 29
  finding character in each plant, 31
  pollarding, 26, *26*
  pruning as an art, 28–29
  using a girdle, 30, *30*
  weeping trees growing upright, 30, *30*, 31
  whips for an allée, 91
Tree tobacco, 11

V

Verbena, *7*
Viburnums, 162, 164
Visual rhythm, 8–9, *9*

W

Weeping Yaupon holly, 109
Wet places, *100*
  amending the soil in, 101–102
  plants for shady, damp areas, 102, 104, *104*, 105
  plants for sunny, damp areas, 102–103, *103*, 104
Wild senna, *116*, 118, 121
Wild strawberry, 98
Willows, 26, *26*, 30, *30*, 142
Winterberry, 144
Winter gardens, *138*, 139–40, *146*, 147–48, *152*, 153
  bark and berry features in, *138*, 140, *140*, 141–42, *143*
  colors in, *141*, 142, *143*, 144, *145*
  crocuses in, 149, *149*, 150
  cyclamen in, *146*, 149, 150, 151
  evergreen features in, 142, *142*, 143, *143*
  flowering shrubs, 150, 151
  hardscape and ornament features in, *143*
  hellebores in, *146*, 147–48, 150, *151*
  ornamental grasses in, 145, 153, 155, *155*, 156–57, 158, *158*, 159, *159*
  perennial accents in, *140*, 144–45
  sculptural backbones for, 140–41, *141*, 142, *142*
  shrubs in, 164
  snowdrops in, 149, 150
  winter-blooming flowers in, *146*, 147, 148, 150, *151*
Winter honeysuckle, 150, 151
Witch hazel, *144*, 145, 150, 151, 161–62, *162*, 163, *163*

Y

Yarrow, 41, *42*, *44*, 45, 46, 118, 121
Yellowroot, 162, 164
Yew, 55
Yucca, 11, *116*, *141*, 145